Praise for *The Imp of the Mind*

LEE BAER, Ph.D., is an internationally recognized expert in
the treatment of OCD and related disorders, and the author of *Getting Control: Overcoming Your Obsessions and
Compulsions* (available in a Plume edition). Dr. Baer is an
associate professor of psychology at Harvard Medical School
and the director of research of the OCD unit at Massachusetts General Hospital, as well as the OCD Institute at
McLean Hospital. He lives near Boston with his wife and
two children.

THE IMP OF THE MIND

EXPLORING THE SILENT EPIDEMIC OF OBSESSIVE BAD THOUGHTS

Lee Baer, Ph.D.

A PLUME BOOK

This book is not intended to replace personal medical care and supervision. There is no substitute for the experience and information that a professional familiar with Obsessive-Compulsive Disorder can provide. Rather, it is hoped that this book will supplement the help that a professional can provide and prove of assistance to those without current access to a professional experienced in this disorder.

To protect privacy, pseudonyms have been used and certain characteristics have been disguised in the case histories recounted.

PLUME
Published by the Penguin Group
Penguin Group (USA) Inc., 375 Hudson Street, New York, New York 10014, U.S.A.
Penguin Group (Canada), 90 Eglinton Avenue East, Suite 700, Toronto, Ontario,
Canada M4P 2Y3 (a division of Pearson Penguin Canada Inc.)
Penguin Books Ltd., 80 Strand, London WC2R 0RL, England
Penguin Ireland, 25 St Stephen's Green, Dublin 2, Ireland
(a division of Penguin Books Ltd.)
Penguin Group (Australia), 250 Camberwell Road, Camberwell, Victoria 3124,
Australia (a division of Pearson Australia Group Pty. Ltd.)
Penguin Books India Pvt. Ltd., 11 Community Centre, Panchsheel Park,
New Delhi – 110 017, India
Penguin Group (NZ), 67 Apollo Drive, Rosedale, North Shore 0632, New Zealand
(a division of Pearson New Zealand Ltd.)
Penguin Books (South Africa) (Pty.) Ltd., 24 Sturdee Avenue,
Rosebank, Johannesburg 2196, South Africa

Penguin Books Ltd., Registered Offices: 80 Strand, London WC2R 0RL, England

Published by Plume, a member of Penguin Putnam Inc.
Previously published in a Dutton edition.

First Plume Printing, March 2002

30

Copyright © Lee Baer, 2001
All rights reserved

℗ REGISTERED TRADEMARK—MARCA REGISTRADA

The Library of Congress has catalogued the Dutton edition as follows:
Baer, Lee.
The imp of the mind : exploring the silent epidemic of obsessive bad thoughts /
Lee Baer.
p.   cm.

Includes bibliographical references.
ISBN 978-0-525-94562-8 (hc.)
978-0-452-28307-7 (pbk.)
1. Obsessive-compulsive disorder—Popular works.   I. Title.

RC533 .B245 2001
616.85'227—dc21
00-041072

Printed in India
Original hardcover design by Leonard Telesca

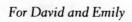

For David and Emily

Acknowledgments

I am pleased to express my gratitude to several groups of people without whom this book would not exist. First, I thank all my patients who suffer with bad thoughts, who have shared their most private secrets with me, and have taught me most of what I know about this problem. I have been touched by the strength of those who have seen improvements in their problem with the treatments described in this book, as well as the courage and good humor of those who remain harshly afflicted, but are nonetheless determined to have the highest quality lives possible despite their problem. I pledge to keep searching for more effective treatments to better assist all of you. I am particularly indebted to all those sufferers of bad thoughts who have shared their experiences with me over the years.

As always, I am indebted to my talented coworkers at Massachusetts General Hospital and McLean Hospital for providing a stimulating work environment and for always being there for support and guidance. I thank Sabine Wilhelm for agreeing to be interviewed about the new developments in cognitive therapy. She, Nancy Keuthen, and Deb Osgood-Hynes graciously provided me with numerous examples of therapy assignments they have used with their patients. Bill Minichiello and Mike Jenike have been my friends and mentors for almost twenty years, and I thank them both for agreeing to be interviewed on religious obsessions and medication treatments, respectively. I thank Cary Savage for agreeing to share in depth his expertise in the neuropsychology and neurophysiology of obsessions. Scott Rauch has sharpened my thinking through many hours of discussion about the overlap between OCD and Tourette's syndrome, and Beth Gershuny called my attention to the fascinating link between post–traumatic stress disorder and obsessions. I thank my psychology colleagues, Mark Blais and Bill Lenderking, for leading our team in developing the quality of life scale included in the final chapter, which is named for Ken Schwartz—a friend lost too young to cancer. I thank our chief of psychiatry at Mass General, Ned Cassem, for his friendship and support over the years, and for giving permission for reprinting the Schwartz Outcome Scale in these pages. Finally, Linda Leahy provided invaluable support in typing the transcripts of many interviews, and searched far and wide for critical research references.

Many colleagues outside of Mass General have contributed to my research in this area. Kathy Wisner in Cleveland gave generously of her time to share her experiences with postpartum obsessions in new mothers in several interviews and E-mail exchanges. Finally, Isaac Marks in London is always available to discuss new treatment approaches—it was he who first called my attention to the early studies of cognitive therapy for obsessions—as well as evolutionary approaches to understanding these and other psychiatric disorders.

At Dutton I thank Deb Brody for first seeing the value of a book on bad thoughts and for encouraging me in pursuing this project. Amanda Patten at Plume stepped in to provide her guidance during the early stages of this project. Finally, Mitch Hoffman, my present editor at Dutton, has made this book far better than it would otherwise have been, through his incisive questions and his wise editing.

Of course this book would not exist at all without the emotional support of my wonderful family. My wife Carole Ann, my son David, and my daughter Emily are the best things in my life, and as usual they were always there to pick me up and carry me through when I was certain this book would never be finished. It is the time I spend with them that recharges me after the hard work of writing and rewriting. My mother, Bernice, and my brother, Larry, have always been strong supporters. The memories of my father Bill, my grandfather Dave, and my grandmother Mary are always with me for inspiration.

As I finish thanking many of those who helped me in the preparation of this book, I take this opportunity to warn that any errors that have found their way onto the following pages are my responsibility alone.

Contents

Preface   xiii

PART ONE: THE PROBLEM OF BAD THOUGHTS

1: The Imp of the Perverse   3

2: Thoughts of Harming Children   19

3: How Can I Be Certain They're Just Thoughts?   31

4: What Causes Bad Thoughts?   45

PART TWO: TREATMENT OF BAD THOUGHTS

5: Facing Your Fears Head-on: Exposure Therapy   73

6: Questioning Your Bad Thoughts: Cognitive Therapy   91

7: Blasphemous Bad Thoughts   106

8: Medications for Bad Thoughts   113

9: A Plan of Action   123

Notes   138

Index   146

Preface

Ever since Sally, a new mother in her midtwenties, had brought her infant daughter, Jessie, home from the hospital, she had become increasingly afraid of being alone with her. Now, when she has to take care of her daughter alone, she thinks about how easy it would be to throw her defenseless Jessie against a wall and smash her skull, or how quickly she could smother her under her tiny pillow. If Sally sees a knife on the kitchen counter, the image of stabbing Jessie floods her mind, disgusting her and filling her with guilt. Her husband, Jack, finds it odd that Sally always prefers that *he* change Jessie's diaper, and that *he* give her a bath, while Sally tries to stay as far away as possible. But so far, she can't bring herself to admit to Jack the awful thoughts that dominate her mind, lest he think her an unfit mother. Even admitting these thoughts to me feels shameful and disgusting to Sally. "No other mother could have thoughts like these—I must be insane," she tells me through her tears.

When I assure her that her thoughts are not nearly as rare as she believes, and that I am not in the least concerned that she will act on them, Sally is slightly relieved, but also puzzled: "How can you be so certain I'm not deep down a murderer who won't one day snap and kill Jessie?" she asks. But the very facts that she feels guilty and worries about having such awful thoughts, and that she has never physically harmed anyone before, are all the clues I need to be able to reassure her that she is not a murderess, but rather one of millions of people who suffer in silence from bad thoughts.

What do I mean by "bad thoughts"? I mean something specific: thinking the most inappropriate things at the most inappropriate times. These thoughts, urges, and images almost always fall into one of three categories: inappropriate aggressive thoughts, inappropriate sexual thoughts, or blasphemous religious thoughts.

These bad thoughts sometimes involve harming an innocent child, urges to jump from the top of a tall building or mountain, urges to jump in front of an oncoming train, or urges to push another person in front of a train or automobile. Some suffer from sexual thoughts they find unacceptable, toward either people they know or strangers—or perhaps even toward religious figures such as God, Jesus, or Mary. Others awaken wondering whether they have incestuous urges, or they worry about urges to say racist things, even those totally contrary to their beliefs.

Because you are reading this book, I assume that, like me, you are curious about why in the world we have such thoughts—the very last things we would want—so I will explore in detail the current thinking about why we have these thoughts; in particular, what causes them, and what goes on in our brains while we experience them.

In the pages that follow, I explain the variety of bad thoughts that my patients experience, and the disorders that can elevate them to serious problems (particularly obsessive-compulsive disorder and depression—postpartum and otherwise). These thoughts are far more common than we usually believe, ranging from mild bad thoughts that just about everyone admits to having occasionally, up to severe bad thoughts (which research that I will discuss later suggests may be endured by millions of adults). Tragically many adolescents also suffer from these serious bad thoughts, often convincing them that they are morally bad people who really want to have sex with their parents or do something equally abhorrent to them. Sadly, as children we rarely learn about how our minds work, either in school or in the family, leaving us open to dangerous misunderstandings later on.

Perhaps you or someone you love has suffered from extreme "bad thoughts," either briefly in the past or continuously over many years. If so, you've probably never told anyone, even a close friend or spouse, about your bad thoughts—terrified that you might be thought insane (and you've probably wondered this very thing yourself!). You probably steer clear of situations that trigger your thoughts and feel shame for having these thoughts in the first place. If you come from a strict religious background, you may worry whether you are already condemned to an eternity in hell—especially if you believe that thinking a thought is as bad as performing the act.

These are obviously not the kinds of thoughts that one discusses in polite cocktail-party conversation. Yet simply learning that thoughts such as these are part of being human, and that similar ones are probably going on in the minds of people you pass on the street every day, should help reassure you that you're not as different as you worry you are. There is help for your thoughts, and they don't have to ruin your quality of life; they can be tamed (a synonym for *tame* is *domesticate*, both of which mean to adapt something to live in intimate association with, and to the advantage of man).

In part two of this book, I explain state-of-the-art treatments that you can try on your own or with a professional to tame your disruptive bad thoughts (including a fascinating series of experiments showing that the more you try to stop your bad thoughts, the stronger you make them).

It would not be unusual for you to have serious concerns that one day you will act on your thoughts, and that deep down you're a criminal. Therefore I will address the challenging question of how you can be certain you will never act upon these thoughts; that is, if you suffer from obsessions, what makes you different from a Susan Smith or a Jeffrey Dahmer, who really do the things you worry about doing. Perhaps most importantly, I hope to help you feel less alone and helpless, and to give you the hope that you can once again find peace of mind.

As a licensed psychologist I am ethically bound to take action if I believe my patient is a danger to others. Yet almost every week some mother tells me she has thoughts of harming her baby, a father tells me he worries he will molest his daughter, and both men and women tell me they think about steering their automobile into an innocent pedestrian or pushing a commuter in front of an oncoming train—yet I take no action. Why? Because experience and research have taught me that these people are not truly dangerous to others. Their thoughts will leave them feeling guilty and depressed and, too often, incapacitated, but their bad thoughts will almost certainly remain just that—bad thoughts.

Over the past twenty years I've become an expert in the treatment of obsessive-compulsive disorder (OCD for short), a neuropsychiatric disorder characterized by upsetting mental obsessions and compulsions such as hand washing or checking door locks. During this time our OCD clinic at Massachusetts General Hospital has grown to be the largest and best known in the world, with past and present patients totaling nearly two thousand. My colleagues Drs. Michael Jenike and William Minichiello and I have coedited the leading textbook on OCD and related disorders, which is currently in its third revision and is used by doctors and medical students around the world.[1] I have also written *Getting Control*, a popular book describing effective behavior-therapy treatment for OCD, which is now available in four languages.[2]

In speaking with my own patients and by corresponding by mail and E-mail with OCD sufferers from as far away as South Africa, Asia, and Australia, I have become fascinated by the large number of patients who have sought my help for their problems and then, in reply to my questions, admitted to violent, sexual, or blasphemous obsessions that they have suffered from in silence, often for years. I am now convinced that this is an underrecognized problem: as an example, a half million American women a year may suffer from horrible thoughts about harming their newborn babies—although they will never do this! Sadly, most of these women never seek treatment, likely because they are so embarrassed by these thoughts that they won't mention them to their doctor or family.

Although people with unacceptable thoughts like these would today be diagnosed with OCD, most of them have not identified themselves with this disorder because they do not wash their hands or check door locks. None of the books that have appeared about OCD in the past decade (including my own *Getting Control*) have focused on these particular mental symptoms—which epidemiological studies around the world suggest may be the *most common* kind of OCD. This is especially unfortunate, since over the past decade we have developed powerful nondrug treatments to effectively treat these intrusive thoughts.

Over the past two years I've conducted a weekly support group at McLean Hospital to try to help sufferers of bad thoughts. It has been gratifying for me to hear participants report that through this group they have learned they are not alone, and that there is hope for recovery. By the same token I've learned a great deal from the participants by listening to their stories, many of which I describe in this book.

To date I've met or treated several hundred people with bad thoughts, and I've noticed two intriguing paradoxes about them:

(1) Nearly everyone who comes to me for help with bad thoughts thinks he or she is the only person with these thoughts. Yet, if everyone in the United States who suffers from these bad thoughts congregated, they would form the fourth-largest city in the United States, with a population exceeded only by those of New York, Los Angeles, and Chicago.

(2) Those suffering from bad thoughts are often more tormented than people with any other psychiatric disorder I have known, and many have contemplated or attempted suicide. Yet, they have almost never told another living soul about the disorder, instead suffering in private.

You could say that I had to write this book to help resolve both of these unfortunate but correctable situations.

The information on the pages that follow recounts the kind of information I would give Sally and similar patients during our meetings: first to help her fully understand her problem with "bad thoughts," and then to help her learn how to tame these thoughts so they no longer cripple her.

The cases I describe on the following pages are experiences of actual patients, or composites of several patients, with all names changed and identities disguised to protect confidentiality. I thank them for sharing their life stories with me.

Boston, Massachusetts
April 2000

THE IMP OF
THE MIND

PART ONE

THE PROBLEM OF BAD THOUGHTS

1

The Imp of the Perverse

One trembles to think of that mysterious thing in the soul, which
seems to acknowledge no human jurisdiction, but in spite of the
individual's own innocent self, will still dream horrid dreams, and
mutter unmentionable thoughts.

—Herman Melville (1819–1891)

I admit it. I can't drive behind a pickup truck with a dog in the
back. Whenever I do, the thoughts start right up. I picture the
dog being thrown off by a bump in the road and being run over by
my car. I try to force the image of the dog crushed beneath my
wheels from my mind, but it's no use. To stop these thoughts, either I speed up and pass the pickup truck, or I slow and drop a few
car lengths behind, until the dog is out of my sight, and hope the
pickup will turn off soon.

Why do I have such thoughts? I know all the psychological and
physiological theories—which I will discuss in detail later—yet
for me, a literary description often captures most vividly what is
happening: Here is none other than my own personal Imp of the
Perverse, perched perhaps upon my right shoulder, whispering
thoughts about running the dog over into my mind's ear. Just who
is my imp? For me, Edgar Allen Poe depicted him perfectly in his
1845 short story "The Imp of the Perverse":

An innate and primitive principle of human action, a
paradoxical something, which we may call *Perverseness*, for

want of a more characteristic term. . . . Through its prompt-ings we act, for the reason that we should *not*. In theory, no reason can be unreasonable: But, in fact, there is none more strong. With certain minds, under certain conditions, it be-comes absolutely irresistible. I am not more certain that I breathe, than that the assurance of the wrong word or error of any action is often the one unconquerable force which impels us, and alone impels us to its prosecution. Nor will this overwhelming tendency to do wrong for the wrong's sake, admit of analysis, or resolution into ulterior elements. It is a radical, a primitive impulse—elementary. . . .

We stand upon the brink of a precipice. We peer into the abyss—we grow sick and dizzy. Our first impulse is to shrink from the danger. Unaccountably we remain. By slow degrees our sickness, and dizziness, and horror, become merged in the cloud of unnamable feeling. By gradations, still more imperceptible, this cloud assumes shape, as did the vapor from the bottle out of which arose the genie in the Arabian nights. But out of this our cloud upon the precipice's edge, there grows into palpability, a shape, far more terrible than any genie, or any demon of a tale, and yet it is but a thought, although a fearful one, and one which chills the very marrow of our bones with the fierceness of the delight of its horror. It is merely the idea of what would be our sen-sations during the sweeping precipitancy of a fall from such a height. And this fall—this rushing annihilation—for the very reason that involves that one most ghastly and loath-some of all the most ghastly and loathsome of images of death and suffering which have ever presented themselves to our imagination—for this very cause do we now the most vividly desire it. And because our reason violently deters us from the brink, therefore, do we the more impetuously ap-proach it. . . .

Examine these and similar actions as we will, we shall find them resulting solely from the spirit of the *Perverse*. We perpetrate them merely because we feel that we should *not*. Beyond or behind this, there is no intelligible principle . . .

Based upon my research and clinical experience with patients, I am convinced that Poe captured a universal human condition in his description of the imp. This phenomenon has been described by others, by various names at various times: the French neurologist Pierre Janet called it "association by contrast," in which the patient feels driven to do precisely the opposite of what he wants to do. Yet, these descriptions, to me, lack the elegance of Poe's.

As I have already admitted, at times my own imp makes his presence felt, through unwanted thoughts and impulses that go counter to the norms of polite society: to swerve my car off the road or to shout an obscenity in public, for example. And few in number are those people who can honestly say that they have never recognized this imp at work in themselves.

Clinical Bad Thoughts

Fortunately, for me, and for most people, these occasional bad thoughts are nothing but a fleeting annoyance. But many people who come to see me are not so fortunate. Their bad thoughts may be about violence or sex or blasphemy and may bombard them every waking hour. These bad thoughts—when severe they are called obsessions—may cost people the most important things in their lives: Some cannot bear to be around their own children; others cannot have relationships; and others are so paralyzed they cannot perform simple everyday activities—such as leaving their house—because of their bad thoughts. Many contemplate suicide at some time. These are obsessions of clinical severity and require treatment.

Just about two years ago I began conducting a group at McLean Hospital for men and women who suffer from clinical bad thoughts. Since that time I have spoken to dozens of patients suffering from these thoughts who've never before admitted them to anyone, but were relieved to find that many other individuals suffer from similar thoughts. The degree to which these bad thoughts have devastated the quality of life of these people has amazed me. Virtually all the people who've come to my group for severe violent or sexual obsessions have thought about suicide, some have even tried suicide, and all have had their social lives disrupted. Some cannot date because of these thoughts; others have been divorced because of the thoughts. Many avoid being around children; most will turn away from television shows, movies, books, magazines, and newspaper accounts of violent or sexual activities, lest they find their own bad thoughts triggered.

Apparently, the Imp of the Perverse visits every one of us from time to time, with two possible outcomes: (1) We give the thoughts little attention and no credence and go on with our lives, or (2) we are strongly affected by the bad thoughts, so that the thoughts occur frequently during the day and interfere with our functioning socially or at work.[1]

An example of the latter outcome was Isaac, a patient of mine in his midtwenties who had always loved animals. Yet by the time I met him he cringed every time he passed a dog or cat on the street. Just a glance at the wagging tail was enough to start the bad thoughts—he felt compelled to stare at the dog's anus and his thoughts would start. They were always the same, thoughts of intercourse with the dog, followed by the worry that this meant he was *really* a pervert. He was often convinced it was true: "Why in the world," he asked himself, "should looking at a dog or a cat on the streets lead me to stare at their private parts or trigger these thoughts about having sex with them—unless that is what I really want?"

After Isaac had told me his story at our first meeting, I told him that if he was to tame his bad thoughts, the first key fact that he had to understand, and believe, was:

You are not so abnormal as you think. Every human being is visited from time to time by the Imp of the Perverse, who makes you think the most inappropriate thoughts at the most inappropriate times.

To help convince Isaac of this, I showed him a list of bad thoughts that were part of a questionnaire given to normal college students in a London study by pioneering psychologist Dr.

Stanley Rachman and his associates. Isaac was surprised when I told him that virtually all of the students said that they had one or more of these thoughts from time to time. I have included part of this list in table 1.

TABLE 1
COMMON BAD THOUGHTS IN HEALTHY COLLEGE STUDENTS

Sexual Impulses or Obsessions

- Thought of acts of violence in sex
- Thought of sexually punishing a loved one
- Thought of "unnatural" sex acts (including sex with animals)
- Impulse to engage in sexual practices that cause pain to the partner
- Sexual impulse toward attractive females, known and unknown
- Impulse to sexually assault a female, known and unknown
- Repetitive blasphemous, obscene images of the Virgin Mary

Violent Impulses or Obsessions

- Thought of causing harm to elderly people
- Wishing or imagining that someone close to one is hurt or harmed
- Impulse to violently attack and kill a dog
- Impulse to violently attack and kill someone
- Thinking or wishing that someone would disappear from the face of the earth
- Impulse to hit or harm someone
- Thought of intense anger toward someone related to a past experience
- Impulse to harm or be violent toward children, especially smaller ones
- Impulse to shout at and abuse someone

Urges or Thoughts About Doing Inappropriate Things in Public

- Impulse to attack and violently punish someone (e.g., to throw a child out of a bus)

- Impulse to say something nasty and damning to someone
- Impulse to say rude and inappropriate things—"wrong thing in wrong place" impulse
- Impulse to push people away or off in a crowd
- Blasphemous thoughts during prayers

Modified from Rachman, S., & de Silva, P. (1978). Abnormal and normal obsessions. *Behaviour Research and Therapy*, 16, 233–248.

Next I told Isaac that not only are these bad thoughts universal among all humans *today*, but they have almost certainly *always* been a part of the human condition, at least since man first developed language and then rules to govern appropriate behavior in groups.

An early reference to something resembling the Imp of the Perverse (i.e., the human curiosity and inability to stop thinking about the very thing we are told not to do) is the Greek myth of Pandora: In bestowing their gifts on Pandora, the gods of Olympus gave her a box, warning her never to open it. But, inevitably, Pandora's curiosity finally overcame her, and she opened the mysterious box, from which flew innumerable plagues and sorrows for humankind. In terror, she tried to shut the box, but only Hope remained inside to comfort humanity against its new misfortunes.

Similarly, in the Judeo-Christian tradition, the biblical story of Eve in the Garden of Eden casts the serpent—here an agent of Satan—in the role of the imp. As soon as God specifically tells Adam and Eve that there is only one tree in the Garden that *they may not even think about eating from*, the release of humanity's troubles (as in the Pandora myth) seems inescapable.

Dr. Ian Osborne, a Penn State psychiatrist, and author of the excellent book *Tormenting Thoughts and Secret Rituals*, recently uncovered two examples of the Imp of the Perverse at work in past centuries. First, there is the record of a sixteenth-century woman who admitted to having evil thoughts about harming her children and her husband, and who barely escaped burning at the stake for these perverse thoughts. This unfortunate woman lived in a time when the Imp of the Perverse was understood—not metaphorically, but in a deadly literal way—as possession by

Satan himself. Only through the intervention of an understanding justice of the peace, who recognized these as "the meaningless intrusive thoughts of a good, but 'melancholy' woman," did she escape burning to expel the "devil" within her.[2]

Nearer to our own time, in the eighteenth century, the patron saint of France, Thérèse of Lisieux, received a letter from her female cousin who wrote about being tormented by horrible sexual obsessions and asking Thérèse for help. Thérèse, who Dr. Osborne notes, probably had obsessions herself, replied reassuringly to her cousin: "You haven't committed the shadow of any evil. I know these kinds of temptations so well that I can assure you of this without any fear. . . . We must despise all these temptations and pay no attention whatsoever to them. . . . Don't listen to the Devil. Mock him." Here again, the imp is thought to be the devil himself, yet Thérèse views him as an annoying and mocking tempter, not one to be deathly afraid of.

How the Imp Selects His Thoughts

A useful rule of thumb I have developed from talking to hundreds of patients with bad thoughts is:

The Imp of the Perverse will try to torment you with thoughts of whatever it is you consider to be the most inappropriate or awful thing that you could do.

To illustrate this point, each of my patients whose thoughts are summarized below (many of whom you'll meet in later chapters) told me that his or her particular bad thoughts focused squarely on whatever was *for him or her* the most inappropriate, awful, or shameful thing he or she could think of doing:[3]

- the man who thought he had killed people while driving
- the woman who worried she'd throw her grandchildren off a bridge

- the new mother who thought she'd poison her infant
- the schoolteacher who thought she'd killed her students
- the doctor who worried about mutilating babies with a scalpel
- the priest who worried about staring at women's private parts
- the woman tormented by thoughts of lesbian sex with her sister
- the man who thought he had sex with people he passed on the street
- the man who feared he would stab children with a knife
- the man who worried he wanted to have sex with animals
- the nun who thought she was damned for having impure sexual thoughts
- the woman who was terrified to go to sleep because the devil would take her for her "bad" sexual thoughts

Can what seems to be the worst possible thing that we can imagine doing change with the passage of time? Absolutely. And a closer look at Isaac's history clearly illustrates this.

Through further questioning I learned that the imp had attacked Isaac at other vulnerable points earlier in his life. When he was an adolescent—although he was heterosexual—the worst possible thing Isaac could think of was being gay, which could cause relentless teasing by his classmates in school. So this is where the imp began his torment of Isaac. Perhaps he would stare at an attractive female classmate and feel pleasantly aroused; but the imp would lead him to think that perhaps it was really the *boy sitting next to her* that he was really attracted to. Soon, whenever he saw an attractive boy in school or on the street or in the gym, he would find himself scanning his body to *try to feel certain* that he wasn't sexually aroused.[4] "Was that the first tingling of an erection?" he'd ask himself. Of course, simply thinking about the area would sensitize it, which might be enough to convince him that he really was homosexual. He might then go home and lie in bed, depressed and thinking about suicide, certain that his classmates would soon discover the truth and begin teasing him mercilessly.

But after a year or two of this, something amazing happened: Isaac realized that he had many friends who were gay, and it no longer seemed a big deal to him whether he was teased about this or not. Since being gay was no longer the most embarrassing and inappropriate thing he could think of doing, the Imp of the Perverse changed his plan of attack: It was now time to torment Isaac with another bad thought.

At this time, for Isaac was now a liberal college student, the worst thing he could think of would be to be a racist. So now, if he saw an African-American walking toward him on the street, the urge would come to shout "Nigger!" Although he was able to fight it off, it stayed in his mind and tormented him. Did it mean he really was deep down a racist? He didn't want to believe it, but maybe it was true. He hated these thoughts, which continued for a couple of years. Finally, one day, Isaac realized he was not a racist, and soon the thoughts no longer seemed real; then one day, they were gone. But the Imp of the Perverse was not through with Isaac yet.

At this time, to Isaac, anyone who had sex with animals was the lowest form of life—beneath his contempt, and of course, this is where the Imp of the Perverse now struck. This is how the obsession that had brought him to our clinic had begun.[5] And it seemed the worst of all. By now it seemed safest simply to stay in his house and take no chances. The imp almost had Isaac beaten. Fortunately, he was soon to turn the tables, but that is getting ahead of our story.

Thought Suppression

For some people, the way they react to the Imp of the Perverse can determine whether their bad thoughts will reach clinical severity, requiring treatment.

For example, Father Jack, a priest in his late fifties, came to our clinic several years ago for help with inappropriate sexual obsessions that threatened to ruin his professional and personal life. For him, the worst thing he could imagine doing would be to be caught staring at a young woman's private parts. Naturally, his personal Imp of the Perverse chose to torment him at this vulnerable point.

Seeing an attractive young woman walking down the street or talking with a female parishioner one-on-one, the priest would have the thought and urge to stare at her buttocks, breasts, or crotch. Over the years he fought this urge with all his strength, but with little success. So he finally found his way to our clinic to seek treatment. Here are parts of the story he told me.

Despite his attempts, the priest found himself staring at a woman's breasts as she walked toward him on the street. He tried to avert his gaze, but as usual, the more he tried, the more he was aware of her, now noticing her breasts bounce as she approached. He finally willed himself to look away until she was past him, but then, against his will, he turned to stare at her shapely buttocks as she walked away. He prayed that people hadn't noticed him staring at her. Had they? If so, what did they think of him, a man of God, ogling a strange young woman's private parts? Would they think him a pervert or rapist?

He turned forward, resolving to keep his eyes focused only on the pavement as he made his way to see me at the hospital, to discuss these vulgar thoughts that plagued him so. "There, that's better," he thought. "If I just keep my eyes downcast, it will be okay." This worked for about a city block, until he looked up again, his gaze fixing on a young woman, alternating between her breasts and crotch. And then the images of having sexual relations with her flooded his mind, filling him with guilt and disgust. Despite his strongest efforts, he was staring at a woman again, he couldn't help it, and he knew that she had noticed. Would she call a policeman? Would she run? If only he could break free from her grip, but it was no use: He was fascinated, compelled to stare at her private parts. The guilt rose, until she was safely past. Mustering all his strength, he resisted the pull to turn around and look at her again. Two more blocks and he'd be safe, in my office, for a change confessing *his* sins to another.

Father Jack tells me he used to deaden the thoughts by drink. But because it had taken larger and larger amounts of alcohol to do this, he had stopped drinking years ago. But now he had no defense left against the thoughts. Was it, he wondered at times, the devil mocking him? Some days he felt certain of this. Who else could taunt him with feelings and thoughts so strong, so unbearable?

He had been but a teenager when the thoughts began. When he had told his superior about them, he was told they would pass with time, and to be patient. Only they didn't. It wasn't that he had trouble maintaining his vow of chastity—that he was sure he could do. Rather, it was the vulgar images that played over and over in his mind, and the way he felt compelled to stare at women's private parts. The very thing he was most afraid of doing—the very thing that seemed most disgusting to him—why was he having these very thoughts and urges?

No one who saw him performing ceremonies in his church knew the torment going on inside his mind. Although he had taken the vow of chastity, his mind refused to cooperate. Finally he confided to a parishioner about the thoughts and images that were forcing themselves into his mind whenever he saw an attractive female on the streets or in church. He soon regretted this confession. He got a call from his superior, who told him about a complaint he had received from a parishioner and a warning that the father might be a dangerous man. Providentially, the superior had heard of obsessive thoughts like Father Jack's, and he arranged for him to receive treatment at our clinic.

Father Jack had been referred to our clinic to participate in a study of medication for obsessive-compulsive disorder. He knew that he had a fifty percent chance of being assigned to take either the active medication or a placebo sugar pill. At the end of our first visit, as I handed Father Jack the bottle of pills he had been assigned by the computer to take in the study, he asked me a question that took me aback. He told me that he had read my book[6] and others about how to deal with obsessions, and he wanted to know if he had understood them correctly: Was it true that the best thing to do was to *stop resisting* his obsessions, and to put himself in the situations that triggered his obsessions, rather than avoid them?

The difficulty for me, I told him, was that because of the rules of the study, I was not allowed to give anyone instructions about using behavior therapy for their symptoms (since behavior therapy is a highly effective treatment for obsessions and compulsions and could invalidate the results of the drug trial). However, I felt obliged to at least tell him that his understanding of the basic principles of behavior therapy were correct—although I could not give him any specific help in using these techniques while the study was going on.

As Father Jack returned for his weekly, and then biweekly, visits, I was pleased to hear that he was feeling better. Apparently the medication was starting to work, and he now noticed that he no longer needed to fight the obsessions or to avoid attractive women on the streets of Boston, since the thoughts passed rapidly through his mind and disappeared.

At the end of the three-month study, when I assessed Father Jack's symptoms using the Yale-Brown Obsessive Compulsive Scale (YBOCS),[7] both he and I were delighted to find that he was the first person in any of our drug studies to that time whose final score was zero. Father Jack returned to his parish, and not until he returned to Boston several months later for a follow-up did he and I learn that he had been taking the placebo throughout the study! To my surprise Father Jack was not upset by this news at all—he told me that he had suspected that his progress was largely due to his decision after our first visit to try his hardest to follow the behavioral principles I had explained in my book. By letting himself look at whatever he wanted to look at; by letting whatever thoughts came simply pass through his mind; by recognizing the bad thoughts as nothing more than thoughts—he had cured himself of his obsessions.[8]

In further discussions, I explained to Father Jack the strong scientific basis for what he had experienced. It is called the "thought to suppression" effect and was introduced by psychologist Daniel Wegner and explained in his excellent book *White Bears and Other Unwanted Thoughts*. College students were instructed to resist thinking about white bears during the experiment. Needless to say, most students had a difficult time keeping the thought of a white bear from intruding in their mind despite their efforts to keep it out. What was more interesting, however, was that after they were told to stop trying to resist thinking about white bears, a rebound effect occurred. That is, after they stopped suppressing thoughts about white bears, these thoughts came into their mind at a higher rate than if they had not tried to suppress these thoughts in the first place.

This certainly seemed to be at least part of Father Jack's problem. The more he fought looking at attractive women, the more he felt compelled to stare at their private parts. This led him to try to avoid streets where he might see attractive women—and as I will explain later, avoiding almost any situation increases our fears of it. In short, Father Jack was trapped in a downward spiral that is common in our patients and is often what leads them to seek treatment with us. Fortunately for Father Jack, simply stopping thought suppression and no longer avoiding places where he would see attractive women were enough to tame his bad thoughts.

What Leads Us to Suppress Bad Thoughts?

Many harbor, but few admit to, the sneaking suspicion that deep down we are really another person, far darker than the polite face we present to other people. For many then, when the Imp of the Perverse visits, and they notice having bad thoughts, these can seem to signal for them the "awakening" of this other, evil part of themselves.

The classic literary description of this fear made real is Robert Louis Stevenson's story *The Strange Case of Dr. Jekyll and Mr. Hyde*. At the conclusion of the story, in confessing his dastardly experiments to his friend, the upstanding citizen Dr. Jekyll writes:

> I was driven to reflect deeply and inveterately on that hard law of life which lies at the root of religion, and is one of the most plentiful springs of distress. Though so profound a double-dealer, I was in no sense a hypocrite; both sides of me were in dead earnest; I was no more myself when I laid aside restraint and plunged in shame, than when I laboured, in the eye of day, at the furtherance of knowledge or the relief of sorrow and suffering. And it chanced that the direction of my scientific studies, which led wholly towards the mystic and the transcendental, reacted and shed a strong

light on this consciousness of the perennial war among my members. With every day, and from both sides of my intelligence, the moral and the intellectual, I thus drew steadily nearer to that truth by whose partial discovery I have been doomed to such a dreadful shipwreck: that man is not truly one, but truly two. I say two, because the state of my own knowledge does not pass beyond that point. Others will follow, others will outstrip me on the same lines; and I hazard the guess that man will be ultimately known for a mere polity of multifarious, incongruous and independent denizens. I, for my part, from the nature of my life, advanced infallibly in one direction and in one direction only. It was on the moral side, and in my own person, that I learned to recognize the thorough and primitive duality of man; I saw that, of the two natures that contended in the field of my consciousness, even if I could rightly be said to be either, it was only because I was radically both; and from an early date, even before the course of my scientific discoveries had begun to suggest the most naked possibility of such a miracle, I had learned to dwell with pleasure, as a beloved daydream, on the thought of the separation of these elements. If each, I told myself, could but be housed in separate identities, life would be relieved of all that was unbearable; the unjust might go his way, delivered from the aspirations and remorse of his more upright twin; and the just could walk steadfastly and securely on his upward path, doing the good things in which he found his pleasure, and no longer exposed to disgrace and penitence by the hands of this extraneous evil. It was the curse of mankind that these incongruous faggots were thus bound together—that in the agonized womb of consciousness these polar twins should be continuously struggling. How, then, were they dissociated?

Sadly, many of my patients, when they first experience violent, sexual, or blasphemous bad thoughts, believe that there is deep down in them—like the ruthless Mr. Hyde living deep within Dr. Jekyll and waiting to be unbound—an evil murderer or molester, their "true" self, whose appearance is heralded by the appearance

of the bad thoughts.[9] For my patients who come to this conclusion, thought suppression seems to them the only logical
approach—that is, to block all attempts of their evil nature from
forcing itself into their consciousness. Sadly, as we now understand, this makes a bad situation far worse (as do artificial attempts to suppress the thoughts by drinking or illegal drugs).

Consequently, another rule of thumb in taming one's bad
thoughts is:

---

*Bad thoughts do not signify that you are truly evil deep
down, and voluntarily suppressing these thoughts will
only make them stronger.*

As a tangible example of the widely different outcomes that
can result from this simple change of outlook, compare the reaction of Father Jack to his bad thoughts with that of a former president of the United States, Jimmy Carter.

While Father Jack viewed his sexual thoughts and urges as evil
and shameful, and needing to be suppressed at all costs, Jimmy
Carter viewed his bad thoughts far differently. In a famous interview in *Playboy* magazine, Carter was asked if his strong religious
beliefs would cause him to be "a rigid, unbending president." His
controversial reply:

> I've looked on a lot of women with lust. I've committed
> adultery in my heart many times. This is something that
> God recognizes that I will do—and I have done it—and God
> forgives me for it. But that doesn't mean that I condemn
> someone who not only looks on a woman with lust but who
> leaves his wife and shacks up with somebody out of wedlock.
> Christ says, don't consider yourself better than someone
> else because one guy screws a whole bunch of women while
> the other guy is loyal to his wife.

Here was Carter, a deeply religious man, a Sunday school
teacher, admitting that he had inappropriate sexual thoughts at

inappropriate times—even admitting that he had broken one of the Ten Commandments. Yet he did not consider these thoughts themselves as shameful, or as something God would punish him for. As a result, he did not suppress such thoughts or avoid situations that triggered them. Had he suffered from either depression or obsessive-compulsive disorder, the effects of these bad thoughts on his life, and on U.S. history, might have been vastly different.

2

Thoughts of Harming Children

Thou shalt not kill.
—The Holy Bible, Exodus 20:15

For most new mothers the most horrible, inappropriate thought they can have is about harming their newborn baby—after all, child killers are reviled even in prison blocks housing the most hardened criminals in our society. It should come as no surprise then that the Imp of the Perverse delights in targeting these precise thoughts to torment these women.

Earlier, you met Sally, who was plagued by bad thoughts about harming her infant daughter, but was too ashamed of these thoughts to tell her husband or her doctor about them. In fact, one of the first questions Sally asked me when we met was whether I had ever heard of any other mother who had horrid thoughts like these about her own baby. She was visibly relieved when I told her that these thoughts are many times more common than most people believe; however, like Sally, most sufferers are too ashamed to tell anyone about the bad thoughts. We are only now beginning to learn how to ask the right questions about this hidden epidemic.

Why do some new mothers brush off occasional thoughts about harming their infant, while others are tormented and may even come to avoid taking care of their child? Apparently, if a new mother is suffering from depression, she is more vulnerable to the influence of the Imp of the Perverse; perhaps her brain is less able to perform its normal function of filtering out bad thoughts such as these, or possibly the negative view of herself that accompanies depression makes her more likely to believe that these thoughts indicate that she is in fact a bad mother.

Bad Thoughts and Postpartum Depression

When new mothers suffer from depression, the disorder is called postpartum depression if it occurs within four weeks after a live birth; if the depression comes on later than four weeks after the birth of a child, it is called simply major depression.

Thoughts of harming one's infant are so common in postpartum depression that in some accounts this is listed as one of the defining elements of this disorder. For example: "Postpartum depression is a living nightmare filled with uncontrollable anxiety attacks, consuming guilt, and obsessive thinking. Mothers contemplate not only harming themselves but also their infants."[1]

One of the first studies to carefully assess these thoughts was beginning several years ago when I received a letter from Dr. Katherine Wisner, a psychiatrist at Case Western Reserve University in Cleveland who specializes in treating women with mood disorders such as depression in the postpartum period (that is, soon after the birth of a child). Dr. Wisner explained in her letter that in her work with women suffering from postpartum depression, she had run across a number of women who, *when asked carefully and in a supportive way*, admitted to also having obsessions about harming their baby; most of these women, she told me, were too ashamed of their thoughts to tell their husbands or obstetricians about them. So Dr. Wisner was planning to conduct a scientific study to determine just how common these bad thoughts were among women suffering from postpartum depression. She was therefore writing to ask my permission to use the self-report questionnaire of common obsessions from my book *Getting Control: Overcoming Your Obsessions and Compulsions*. She reasoned that by showing women a questionnaire including a variety of awful aggressive and sexual obsessions, they would be more likely to be honest in reporting these symptoms if they were truly present. At that time, I had seen a number of women like Sally and was becoming interested in this kind of obsessive thought; thus I wrote back to Dr. Wisner gladly giving her permission to use my questionnaire in her study, and asking her to keep me informed of its results. I was especially interested in her results because she sees patients at the Women's Mood Disorders Clinic in Cleveland, where women are not specifically coming for treatment for obsessions or compulsions, as is the case in the OCD clinic where I work. I thought this feature of her setting would give us a more accurate indicator of just how common these bad thoughts were.

Scientific studies take time to complete carefully, so about two years passed before Dr. Wisner sent me an early draft of her paper to comment on. The study showed that bad thoughts about harming babies were far more common among women suffering from postpartum depression than I had expected.[2] Specific examples of their obsessions are listed in table 2.

TABLE 2
OBSESSIONS ABOUT HARMING BABIES IN POSTPARTUM DEPRESSION

- putting the baby in the microwave
- drowning the baby
- stabbing the baby
- throwing the baby down the stairs or over a railing
- images of the baby lying dead in a casket
- seeing the baby's head bleeding, cracked by a ceiling fan
- images of baby being eaten by sharks

Modified from Wisner et al.[3]

How can we be certain that these thoughts were simply irrational obsessions rather than homicidal urges on the part of these women? (Or as one of my patients put it: "How can I be sure I am not going to end up like Susan Smith, who drowned her children in a car?") This crucial question will be explored in the following chapter. For now, however, some vital clues from Dr. Wisner's findings make it clear that the Imp of the Perverse was at work in causing these women their dreadful thoughts. Not only did the women in the postpartum-onset group experience an elevated rate of thoughts of harming their baby, but they also reported experiencing the following thoughts: fear of doing embarrassing things (32%), fear of terrible things happening (22%), blasphemous obsessions (19%), fear of something being wrong with their body (16%), fear of harming themselves (11%), fear of blurting out obscenities (11%), sexual obsessions (8%), and the fear of stealing (3%). These are clearly the thoughts of women worrying about doing the most inappropriate thing at the most inappropriate time! To get a better idea of what these women told Dr. Wisner about their experiences, I asked her whether the women described their bad thoughts as urges to harm their baby or if they described worrying that they could possibly do this. The women in her study told her that "they did not so much have an 'urge' to hurt the baby, but rather the fear that they might 'lose control' and hurt the baby. For example, one woman would worry that while cutting a tomato she would 'somehow' lose control of her actions and stab the baby; another worried that she would have a 'lapse of consciousness' and not remember poisoning her baby."

Dr. Wisner's findings permit us to calculate a partial estimate of how common these bad thoughts may be. Using a conservative estimate of a ten percent prevalence of postpartum depression, and assuming that half of these women have aggressive obsessions, we can estimate that perhaps five percent of new mothers suffer from aggressive obsessional thoughts toward their babies. Therefore, in the United States, where roughly 4 million babies are born each year, 200,000 new mothers may develop disturbing obsessions about harming their newborns. Based on her experience, Dr. Wisner agrees this estimate is realistic. Of course it doesn't take into account those women who are bothered by these thoughts who *do not* suffer from postpartum depression (these are described later in this chapter).

To make matters worse, we can assume that few of these women will tell their husbands or doctors about these thoughts, instead suffering in silence. Dr. Wisner told me: "In my experience, women are very reluctant to tell anyone, even their husbands, about their obsessions. They almost never tell their obstetricians because they fear being thought of as 'crazy.' They often do not directly tell us either, until we ask the questions in a matter-of-fact way; then they often start crying and ask us, 'How did you know?' "

Dr. Wisner told me about her experiences with women who become more depressed because of how they interpret their obsessions: "Am I having these thoughts because I am a bad mother?" "Does this mean I really did not want to have this baby?" "Do I have some unresolved childhood problems which may make me capable of hurting my baby?" "If I tell anyone about these thoughts, will my baby be taken from me?" Interpretations like these are sure to worsen any postpartum depression that the new mother is already experiencing, making her even *more* likely to have bad thoughts about her baby.

Depression After the Postpartum Period

Of course, the Imp of the Perverse does not end his siege on new mothers after the arbitrary three-month postpartum period is over. Several recent studies have described mothers' thoughts of harming their children as old as three years.

Recently Dr. Jennings and associates at the Western Psychiatric Institute and Clinic in Pittsburgh asked one hundred clinically depressed women with at least one child under three years of age about any obsessions they might have of harming their child. Of these depressed mothers, forty-one (41%) admitted to having such thoughts. Many of these women admitted that they were afraid of being left alone with their child, and for some, these fears left them unable to care for their child. As a comparison group, these researchers also asked forty-six nondepressed mothers the same questions and found that "only" seven percent admitted to thoughts of harming their child.[4] (Although significantly lower than the rate for depressed mothers, at this rate, an additional 280,000 nondepressed American women each year would develop obsessions about harming their children.)

And not only the mothers of very young children suffer from these bad thoughts. Kay, a professional woman in her forties, came to see me for relief of appalling thoughts about stabbing her teenage children as they slept. Kay described to me a night alone with her sleeping children: Her son and daughter were sleeping upstairs when the thought that she might stab them came into her mind. Kay's glance fixed on a long steak knife lying on the kitchen counter, and she felt her blood run cold as she pictured herself plunging it deep into her innocent girl. She told me how she pictured her daughter's crimson blood staining dark red the white cotton sheets. She described picturing her daughter's eyes flying open not comprehending, jarred from the confusion of half-sleep to seeing her trusted mother betraying her. Despite her efforts to force the thoughts from her mind, Kay imagined her son in the next room, awakened now and paralyzed with fear by his sister's cries. Kay next imagined herself moving swiftly to his room, the long steak knife now raised directly over his chest, ready to plunge, and then . . . Finally, Kay succeeded in tearing her gaze from the steak knife on the kitchen counter. She told herself she mustn't allow herself to think these things—not while her husband was away and she was alone with the children. Finally, Kay described to me feeling the cold sweat on her brow and upper lip as she wiped her face with a trembling hand.

After Kay finished describing this incident, and the terror she commonly felt when alone with her teenage children, we discussed the history of her problem further. We agreed that it was odd she had these fears and bad thoughts now, when her children were older, but not before when the children were much younger and far more vulnerable. Kay told me that when her children were younger, she had divorced their father—her first husband—ending an unhappy marriage in which she had suffered emotional and physical abuse. Not until she had recently remarried and had a happy, secure relationship with a caring man did her obsessions about harming her children begin. Kay, an insightful woman, concluded, "It seems as if it's when things are going well for me, almost too well, that my mind has to come up with something to ruin it, something for me to worry about. As if this happiness can't go on, and I fear that I will do something awful to spoil it."

Although we cannot know with certainty why Kay's obsessions began when her children were much older, their occurrence at a time when she finally felt her life was going wonderfully fits with what many other patients have told me. Over the years I have seen many other people like Kay who only had bad thoughts when things were going—in their words—"too well."

Grandmothers' and Aunts' Bad Thoughts

The Imp of the Perverse is not particular in whom he torments with thoughts about harming babies. Apparently anyone who is around babies and has some responsibility for taking care of them is fair game.

Ginny was an accomplished professional in her fifties. She had confided in her doctor about her bad thoughts about harming her grandchild, and the doctor had referred her to me for help. Although Ginny loved her granddaughter and loved nothing more than to baby-sit for her, doing so now kept her awake the night before, and obsessions about harming the baby had robbed her of any pleasure in the baby-sitting.

In our first session, Ginny explained that anytime she was alone baby-sitting for her grandchild, her obsessions would begin. If she was outside, pushing the baby in her stroller, the thought might come: "What if I get the urge to push the stroller in front of a car and kill her?" If she was walking over a bridge near her home, she would imagine throwing the baby over the side of the bridge to her death in the waters below. If she stayed inside with the baby to try to avoid these thoughts, she would instead be assaulted with worries about throwing the baby to her death out the window or suffocating her in her bed (the Imp of the Perverse is nothing if not resourceful). These thoughts were agonizing for Ginny, who was psychologically sophisticated and had good insight into the cause of her obsessions.

Ginny told me that, like Dr. Wisner's patients, her problem was not so much that she had an urge to kill her grandchildren, but rather a fear that she might somehow lose control of her senses. She put it this way: "The fear is not that in my current state I would do these things, but that I might slip into a state where I could do it. Right now, when I am thinking about it, I know it won't happen. But still it festers, it festers and lingers, and it keeps beating on you and beating on—like it's the villain, the enemy, the monster, the demon—it's a faceless devil."

With my encouragement, Ginny told her husband about the thoughts. She was relieved that his reaction was "he just couldn't even believe what he was hearing—he knew I'd never do these things, they were just bad thoughts." When I asked Ginny why she thought he has so much faith in her, she replied, "Because he sees me with people daily. He said he fell in love with me because I am kind. For example, he reminded me of a time when we were together in a cabin, and I noticed a bee trapped behind a screen and I told him I didn't want the bee to die, so he spent the first hour of our first weekend together undoing the screen to free the bee. He asked me, does that sound like someone who would kill her grandchildren? He also reminded me that I am soft and warm and very loving, and he would never worry about me doing the awful things I was thinking of." Needless to say, Ginny was relieved by her husband's reaction, since she had feared he would think she was crazy.

I will explain in a later chapter how Ginny was able to so tame these bad thoughts that she can now be around her grandchildren with no obsessions at all. But that is getting ahead of the story. For now, I want to point out how it is not only mothers who have bad thoughts about harming children.

Ginny provided another example of this recently when she told me about a brief stay with her sister and her sister's baby, when to her surprise her bad thoughts recurred. She told me in detail about what had happened when she was left alone and, in her eyes, responsible for this infant boy she had met just once before:

I was taking the baby out for a ride in the stroller, and the top was up and he had a blanket and hat on him while he was sleeping. Suddenly I became afraid that he couldn't breathe, and then I remembered hearing that sudden infant death syndrome is often mistaken for someone smothering the baby. And I immediately thought, "What if something snaps in my mind and this becomes not just an obsession, but I actually smother him?" The rest of the time I was with him, if his hat or blanket fell over his face slightly, I would rush to put it back before he smothered. I didn't have images of smothering him or urges to smother him. There was just that dastardly voice saying: "What if you did that?" or "Wouldn't it be awful if you smothered him?" But at the intellectual level I knew that I would never do it. I didn't tell my sister because she would have been horrified, and she would probably not have let me around the baby. Believe it or not, when I got off the airplane back at home, I kept waiting for someone to telephone and tell me that the baby had been smothered!

Ginny thought my metaphor of the Imp of the Perverse described her experience well. It also reminded her of two other bad thoughts that had troubled her:

- Recently when she was ordering a cake for a baby shower, she had the urge to tell the baker to write on it "I hope you have an abnormal baby."
- When she used to change her grandchildren's diapers, she used to get the thought "I don't want to look at their sexual organs, because what if something snaps in my mind and I sexually molest them?"

Once again, thoughts such as these are the calling cards of the Imp of the Perverse. They are not the homicidal thoughts of a dangerous woman, but rather the fear of doing the most inappropriate thing at the most inappropriate time.

Although sexual obsessions about one's children, such as Ginny told me about, are less commonly reported than aggressive obsessions, I have seen a number of women who had these bad thoughts. Martie, a woman in her midtwenties, recently told me that she has to force herself to bathe her two-year-old son. She fears that seeing him naked in the bath might lead her to lose control and touch his genitals improperly. Like most other patients who have told me about fears of sexually abusing children, Martie also has fears about harming her son in some other way, such as suffocating him with a pillowcase or stabbing him with a knife. Her sexual obsessions seem to be simply one other manifestation of the Imp of the Perverse: Since the only thing she can conceive of doing that would be as awful as killing her son is to sexually abuse him, this is precisely what the imp selects to torment her with.

For a long time, no reports had been published of such sexual obsessions about one's own children, likely because such thoughts are even less rarely admitted to than violent obsessions. Recently however, two English researchers described two new mothers suffering from these thoughts.[5] Drs. Brockington and Filer, of the Mother and Baby Unit at the Queen Elizabeth Psychiatric Hospital in Birmingham, noted that since sexual obsessions are present in more than one-quarter of all people suffering from obsessive-compulsive disorder, we would expect at least some mothers to obsess about sexually abusing their children. They then described the only two cases of young mothers in the medical literature to date who experienced obsessional thoughts of sexually abusing their own children. To demonstrate how bizarre sexual obsessions can become in some mothers, Dr. Brockington told me of a case he and his colleagues have seen of a pregnant woman obsessed with sexually abusing the unborn fetus. Like obsessions about killing one's baby, sufferers can recognize that these thoughts are ridiculous when they are calm and away from their child. Yet, when alone with their baby—which they usually try to avoid—they feel extreme fear that they might snap and act on these thoughts.

Men's Bad Thoughts About Children

Although the emphasis in this chapter has been upon women and their urges to harm or sexually abuse their children, I do not want to give the impression that men are immune from such thoughts. Far from it. I have seen several men, both with children and without, who are tormented by such thoughts. Several married men have told me that, although they have never admitted it to their wife, they have continued to delay having children because of their fears of harming a newborn.

Gary, a deeply religious man in his thirties, came to see me for help with tormenting obsessions about sexually abusing his young daughter or her friends. He described a recent episode of his bad thoughts this way:

> I was driving my daughter Jane and her best friend, Katie, home, and the two seven-year-old girls were singing and joking and having a good time—it was great. But then the awful thoughts came into my head once again: "How can you be sure you don't *really* want to rape Katie?" The thought disgusted me. I told myself, "I don't want to molest her!" But my thoughts asked, "How can you be absolutely certain?" and "For that matter, how can you be sure you haven't *already* done it!" This really freaked me out.
>
> I was only vaguely aware of the girls talking to me, asking why I was driving so slowly, but I was too upset to answer them. As I tried to remember *not* having raped Katie the graphic image formed in my mind of having sexually molested her! I tried to force the image from my mind, but it continued, and I began to feel sick to my stomach. Then, the image turned into the one that I dread most in the world—molesting my own daughter! Why me, who is revolted by mention of any kind of sexual molestation? Surely I must be destined for hell.
>
> Finally, the thoughts passed, but I knew I would still be shaky for several days, keeping my distance from my little girl, until the aftershock of having these horrible thoughts slowly subsided. What if my wife ever found out?

Gary, like most men with such thoughts, suffered in silence with them for years before seeking help. When he spoke to me, he had still not told his wife the details of his obsessions, for fear that she would divorce him and prevent him from ever seeing his daughter again. It is impossible to estimate how many men suffer from obsessions of physically or sexually harming young children, since men are less likely to seek treatment for any psychological problem than are women. In many of the cases I have seen, the men came into treatment for alcohol or drug addictions they had developed in unsuccessful attempts to self-medicate their obsessions. Only much later, when they learn that their violent or sexual obsessions toward children are not uncommon or criminal, will they sometimes admit to these thoughts. In recent groups, I have seen a couple of men who abused alcohol to try to deaden their obsessions. One was a teacher who worried that he would, or that he already had, unknowingly sexually abused his male students; another worried that he would stab young children he was left alone with. (In a rare event, when this man told his wife about his obsessions, she was unable to accept them as obsessions and asked for a divorce, telling him that she could never trust him to be around any children they might have. Happily nearly all spouses are a lot more understanding of their partners' irrational obsessions.)

In the next chapter we turn to the fundamental question of how you can be certain that the bad thoughts you are suffering from are simply irrational fears caused by the Imp of the Perverse. After all, anyone who watches the evening news or reads a daily newspaper knows that some people (mercifully very few) do kill or sexually attack children. If no one ever did these things, then there would be no reason to worry about having bad thoughts. As Sigmund Freud pointed out, there would be no need for "Thou shalt not . . ." taboos or Commandments if mankind did not occasionally act on its primal instincts. Thankfully, as you will see, the two facts that, (1) you are upset by your bad thoughts, and (2) that you have never acted on them, are sure signs that you will never act on them.

3

How Can I Be Certain They're Just Thoughts?

> There is no such thing as absolute certainty, but there is
> assurance sufficient for the purposes of human life.
>
> —John Stuart Mill (1806–1873)

Although I try to reassure my patients that people who experience distressing bad thoughts like theirs do not act on them, I can understand their horror at having such thoughts. After all, if babies were never killed by their parents, then thoughts about harming infants would easily be recognized as ridiculous—but sadly we live in a world in which babies are murdered, and most often at the hands of their own parents. As an example, a recent newspaper account described a teenaged mother who was charged with killing her one-month-old son by putting him in a microwave oven and turning it on. While she awaited trial, she was held without bail in a psychiatric hospital.[1]

Imagine the fear that reading an article like this strikes in the heart of a new mother like Sally, whom we met earlier, who suffers alone with worries about harming her infant child.

The news media serve us a regular diet of sensational stories about the dangers surrounding us. For example, a recent cover of *Sports Illustrated* magazine carried the ominous title "Who's Coaching Your Kid? The frightening truth about child molestation in youth sports" above mug shots of eight male coaches convicted of sexually molesting adolescents who had been entrusted to their care.[2] This article provided a valuable service by warning parents about truly dangerous men who might prey upon their children. Amazingly, the article reported that "the average 'preferential' molester, the kind most common in youth sports, victimizes about 120 children before he is caught."

As a parent (and Little League coach) I take to heart the guidelines suggested by the *Sports Illustrated* article for checking out the coaches that I entrust my children to. On the other hand, I have also seen the impact this sort of story can have on a man tormented by fears that he might one day sexually abuse children— *when every bit of evidence suggests that he will never act upon his bad thoughts.* No wonder the majority of patients in my groups for severe bad thoughts tell me that they have contemplated suicide. "Sometimes I am certain that I am not fit to live in normal society" is a common refrain for many of my patients. While I agree that this sentiment certainly is true for the child molesters described in the magazine article, (some of whom are serving prison sentences of up to eighty-four years), this does *not* apply to the man tormented by doubt and guilt over bad thoughts—thoughts that he is no more likely to act upon than I am. My patients with bad thoughts are unable to draw this crucial distinction.

Almost without exception, people who suffer from disturbing bad thoughts are never quite convinced that they won't one day snap and act upon them. After the shooting at Columbine High School in Colorado, some of my patients with violent obsessions worried that they might one day act on their thoughts and tormented themselves worrying that *they* might become the next Columbine High School killers.

Several years ago, when the trial of Susan Smith was in the news, many women with obsessions about harming their children were horrified to learn about this seemingly normal mother who could lock her children in her car, strap them in, and then watch as the car sank into a lake. The question I heard most often was "How can I be sure that I won't end up like Susan Smith?"

A recent book about the evil acts humans have performed, *Dark Nature*, described the chilling scenario this way:

On the night of October 25, 1994, Susan Smith put her Mazda car into gear, slammed the door, and let it roll down a boat ramp into a dark country lake in South Carolina. Strapped into the backseat were her two baby sons, the ones nicknamed "Precious" and "Sugar Foot." An hour later, she accused an unknown black man of stealing the car and kidnapping her children at gunpoint, staring in the camera and pleading so that thousands were searching in response to her tearful appeals on national television. But when nothing was found, the investigation turned back on the immediate family, and Susan made a stunning confession. She took police to where the car was and the boys' bodies were found.

The lying and deceit involved produced shock and outrage in a public accustomed to explaining the dangers of strangers to their children, but faced now with the far scarier statistic that, in the United States alone, one thousand children are killed each year by their parents or close relatives. That half of these victims are under the age of one, and most of these are murdered by their mothers.[3]

Similarly, many male patients with violent obsessions, respected pillars of their communities—patients who will never act on their thoughts—worry that they might one day snap and become a mass killer like Jeffrey Dahmer. This question brings me to the central question of this chapter: "How can I be certain these are *only* thoughts?"

Case Study: Uncertainty About Bad Thoughts

Frank was a young man in my group in his midtwenties who illustrated to me the torturous problem of OCD sufferers with bad thoughts. Try as he might, he simply couldn't feel *certain enough* to satisfy himself that he wouldn't one day act on his violent thoughts and end up like Jeffrey Dahmer. By the time Frank had joined my group for people suffering from bad thoughts, he had already been treated by one of my colleagues and had made significant gains. Frank suffered from violent obsessions about stabbing people. He avoided knives and other sharp objects, and his worst fear was that he might one day become like Jeffrey Dahmer. Frank came from a very religious family and was taught—or at the least, learned—that he was *never* to express any angry feelings.

His violent thoughts had begun a few years before, with worries of stabbing a family member. As with most of my other patients with bad thoughts and a strict Christian upbringing, Frank feared that he had already committed an unpardonable sin simply by *thinking* such thoughts and worried that he was already destined for hell. But happily, with exposure treatments at our clinic such as holding knives and viewing loop tapes of his worst fears described in his own words, and by learning how to better control his anger, Frank was much better. He was now able to work, with his bad thoughts coming only occasionally.

Yet Frank still tried to feel completely *certain* that he would not one day become a mass murderer like Jeffrey Dahmer. Part of Frank's treatment had been to watch a filmed biography of Dahmer over and over until it had lost its ability to frighten him and became, simply, boring. Having OCD, and tending to see things as either black or white and in perfectionistic terms, as well as being overconscientious, he was extremely hard on himself and insisted that he somehow be guaranteed that he would not one day snap and act on his thoughts. At one point, Frank told me that he was now concerned that he was feeling *too little* anxiety, which made him think that perhaps he was a sociopath without a conscience after all and *would* end up like Jeffrey Dahmer!

When other group members reminded Frank that no one, tormented by bad thoughts or not, could ever be guaranteed that he would *never* act on his thoughts, Frank agreed that this was logical, and he understood it while he was there in the clinic. However, when he was on his own, he frequently felt a need to try to convince himself completely.

Perhaps with continued cognitive therapy for OCD, as described later in this book, Frank will finally stop his quest for absolute certainty. Until then, Frank continues to work, is learning to express anger appropriately, and is living life again, for the first time in many years.

*   *   *

Discussing certainty with my patients is a precarious balancing act. On the one hand, most are obsessed with the effort to reach absolute certainty that they can never act on their thoughts—and are tormented by the existence of even the slightest doubt. This is always a losing battle, since we cannot be one hundred percent certain of anything—it is not even absolutely certain that the sun will rise tomorrow and is far less certain that I will not commit a murder one day (although I am able to live a relatively sane life knowing this is a minute possibility not worth worrying about).

For patients like Isaac, who fears wanting to have sex with animals, and Martie, who fears wanting to have sex with her young son, their search for certainty leads them to scan their bodies to prove to themselves they are not aroused. Both have told me that when they worry that they really want to act on their obsession, they will check to make sure they do not feel any sexual arousal or "tingling." In every case, this increases their anxiety, because they fail to realize that any sensitive part of our body that we focus all of our attention on will have some feelings, simply due to the increased attention to that area. Try this yourself—focus your attention on your genitals for a few seconds and try to prove to yourself that you feel *absolutely no* sensations there. It should now be obvious that a key part of successfully treating sufferers of bad thoughts such as Isaac and Martie, therefore, lies in getting them to stop checking their bodies for reassurance, since doing so actually decreases their confidence and raises their fear that they "really" want to act on their urges.

To the oft-asked question "How can I be absolutely certain I will never act on my bad thoughts?" my answer is simple: *You can't.* In fact, *the very act* of trying to attain perfect certainty is often the worst source of distress for those suffering from violent, sexual, or blasphemous bad thoughts. It is not coincidental that the French refer to obsessive-compulsive disorder as "the doubting disease," for this is a core feature of the loop my patients are caught in—endlessly seeking reassurance and futilely seeking absolute certainty.

Does everyone suffering from intrusive violent, sexual, or blasphemous thoughts have OCD? Technically, yes. Based upon the official diagnostic criteria of the American Psychiatric Association, anyone with the bad thoughts I have been describing that occur frequently or interfere with his or her life would be diagnosed with OCD (see table 3).

TABLE 3
CHARACTERISTICS OF OBSESSIVE COMPULSIVE DISORDER (OCD)

Either obsessions or compulsions, which are very distressing, take more than one hour a day, or interfere with doing work, school, or social activities.

Obsessions are:
- intrusive and unpleasant thoughts, impulses, or images that are not excessive worries about real life problems
- examples:
  • aggressive obsessions
  • sexual obsessions
  • blasphemous obsessions
  • doubting obsessions
  • contamination obsessions
  • symmetry obsessions
  • perfectionistic obsessions

Compulsions are:
- actions that the person feels driven to do over and over again, either because of an obsession, or according to rigid rules
- the actions are done to reduce distress or to prevent something bad from happening
- examples
  • washing
  • checking
  • repeating
  • praying
  • touching
  • counting
  • hoarding or saving things
  • rearranging or tidying up
  • asking for reassurance

Modified from American Psychiatric Association, *Diagnostic and Statistical Manual of Mental Disorders,* 4th ed. (Washington, D.C.: American Psychiatric Association, 1994).

This permits us to calculate another estimate of how common severe bad thoughts are. In almost every culture that has been studied, the prevalence of OCD is at least two percent of the general population. Further, in these door-to-door epidemiological surveys—unlike in patients who come to us for treatment—the majority have obsessions (or bad thoughts) only. Given these two facts, we can conservatively estimate that one percent of the population suffers from bad thoughts at any time, or more than 2 million sufferers in the United States alone.

Although the Imp of the Perverse shrewdly plants his seed of doubt in places where it can never be totally expunged, I do discuss *some* evidence with my patients at the start of treatment to reassure them that the possibility of their ever acting on their bad thoughts is negligible. Specifically I tell them the crucial differences between them, who suffer from disturbing but harmless bad thoughts, and the infamous people they have read about who have actually committed horrible acts.

As an example, I point out that *the very fact that they have never acted on their thoughts and urges up until now is an excellent predictor that they will never act on them.* A rock-solid axiom of both psychology and criminology is that the best predictor of future behavior is past behavior.[4] Likewise, the mere fact that they feel guilt and distress over their bad thoughts is a powerful indicator that they will not act upon their bad thoughts.

On the other hand, as I acknowledged at the beginning of this chapter, I am not naive enough to believe that no people commit criminal acts. Therefore I am always looking for clues that a patient may be truly dangerous.

Some Warning Signs

I wrote earlier that although my patients often confess thoughts of harming their children or spouse, I don't take action on their thoughts. That is, I don't worry that they will act on these thoughts and become a threat to others. Does that mean that I am not concerned about *any* patients? Absolutely not.

Of the thousands of patients who have passed through our clinic over the past fifteen years, just a handful have concerned me greatly. Here is one example: A young man from another state was referred by his psychiatrist for behavior therapy to expose him to his bad thoughts about harming other people.[5] However, when I met this man and he began telling me about his thoughts, I grew more and more concerned. I tried to reassure myself by asking him many detailed questions to determine whether exposure therapy was indicated for his problem. His answers to my questions raised my level of concern even higher. He told me that he liked to watch appearances on television by public figures such as the pope or the president, and while watching them, he would imagine himself in the crowd, firing a shot at one of these leaders! When he described these experiences, I wasn't convinced that the idea was totally distasteful to him. He also told me about thoughts of stabbing or shooting his parents. He said that he sometimes "tested" himself by standing in their bedroom doorway and pointing an air rifle at them as they slept to "prove" to himself that he wouldn't really pull the trigger. At the conclusion of our interview I told him that behavior therapy wasn't appropriate for his problem, and that instead I was sending him back to his doctor for further testing. Later that day, I telephoned the referring doctor to tell him that I had a gut feeling that his patient could potentially be dangerous, and I recommended a full battery of projective psychological tests in his hometown to rule out psychosis or criminal potential.

What was it about this fellow that made me worry? Partly it was that he didn't feel tormented by, or even particularly guilty about, his bad thoughts. Partly it was that when he spoke about his parents, or about other people in his town, he seemed to express too much anger toward them for slights he perceived that they had committed against him. Partly it was that he had actually picked up a rifle and pointed it at people involved with his bad thoughts. Looking back, I suppose a combination of all these factors made me worry that he could potentially be dangerous and was suffering from a problem far more serious than OCD.

As I write this chapter, new information has surfaced about the teenagers who shot fellow students in an armed raid on Columbine High School in Colorado. In tapes made during the planning of these shootings, a picture comes into focus of these teenagers as enraged adolescents who had been picked upon by other students and were now eagerly planning their revenge. This combination of rage, fantasies about getting back at classmates who teased and excluded them, and easy access to firearms made for a deadly combination.

On the other hand, the patients who come to see me with violent or sexual thoughts present a wholly different picture. They are overly conscientious people who are tormented daily by their bad thoughts. These thoughts generate intense guilt, and indeed they feel sinful when such thoughts pass through their mind.

I tell these patients that the *very fact* that they feel so upset, so ashamed, and so guilty about their thoughts should give them faith that they will never act on their thoughts. Yet typically they are not so easily reassured. When they ask, "How I can be certain that I won't snap one day and murder like Jeffrey Dahmer or Susan Smith or the Columbine high school shooters?" I tell them that the people who engage in these criminal acts usually have precisely the opposite emotions from the guilt and shame my patients feel.

The history of violent crime is dominated by individuals who have at various times been called sociopaths, psychopaths, or simply cold-blooded killers, indicating that they feel no guilt or remorse about their antisocial or criminal behavior. Even when hooked to a lie detector, describing horrible actions or lying, they show little physiological reaction. In short, they don't feel guilty or remorseful about even the most horrible acts they perform. Such individuals typically meet criteria for a diagnosis of Antisocial Personality Disorder when adults, and for Conduct Disorder before they reach age eighteen. Characteristics of these disorders are listed in table 4.

TABLE 4
Characteristics of Conduct Disorder in Children and Antisocial Personality Disorder in Adults

Conduct Disorder (age 14 or younger)	Antisocial Personality Disorder (age 15 or older)
- *is violent or cruel to people or animals* • bullies or threatens others • picks fights • uses a weapon (bat, gun, broken bottle, brick, knife) • steals when confronting a victim • forces others into sexual activity - *destroys property* • sets fires • deliberately destroys property - *lies or steals* • breaks into a house or car • lies or "cons" others • engages in shoplifting or forgery - *seriously disobeys parents' rules (before age 13)* • stays out at night • runs away from home more than once • is often truant from school	- frequently does unlawful things that could lead to arrest - repeatedly lies, cons others, or uses aliases - acts impulsively and doesn't plan ahead - frequently gets into physical fights or attacks - is often reckless, disregards safety of self or others - acts irresponsibly—doesn't pay bills, can't keep a job - lacks remorse, doesn't feel guilty, explains away acts that harm others

These patients are the utter opposites of my patients with bad thoughts, who are overconscientious and feel intense guilt and tremendous distress at having such thoughts. Many patients with bad thoughts would be diagnosed with Obsessive-Compulsive Personality Disorder (which, as Table 5 indicates, is characterized in part by overconscientiousness).

TABLE 5

CHARACTERISTICS OF OBSESSIVE-COMPULSIVE PERSONALITY DISORDER (OCPD)

- Overly conscientious and inflexible about moral and ethical issues
- Preoccupied with details or rules (loses the forest for the trees)
- Perfectionism interferes with getting things done
- Excessively devoted to work
- Trouble throwing worthless things away
- Insists that others submit to his or her way of doing things, and tolerates no deviation
- Lack of generosity
- Rigid and stubborn

Modified from American Psychiatric Association, *Diagnostic and Statistical Manual of Mental Disorders,* 4th ed. (Washington, D.C.: American Psychiatric Association, 1994).

The guilt and distress these patients suffer is the result of the part of their brain called the prefrontal cortex doing its job by energetically suppressing their bad thoughts. I recently asked my colleague Dr. Cary Savage, an expert in the neuropsychology of OCD, what he would tell patients who worry that they might one day act on their urges. "The very fact that they feel guilt and distress about having bad thoughts should reassure them that their orbital frontal cortex is doing its job," he said. "It is working properly to inhibit their thoughts and these urges, so they should have faith that they will not act on them."

So, there is a vast difference between my patients who feel intense guilt and shame about their violent or sexual thoughts and those who commit crimes coolly and feel no guilt or remorse. To make this distinction clearer, think back to the patient Sally, whom you met in the preface. She was horrified by thoughts that she might snap and harm her infant—thoughts that caused her intense shame and guilt. Contrast Sally with Susan Smith, who strapped her two boys into their car seats, coolly watched as the car rolled into a lake, then watched them struggle to escape before they finally drowned. Indeed, she was *so cool* and felt so little guilt that only a few hours later she was standing in front of a television camera lying convincingly about a black man who, she said, had kidnapped her children, pleading with the audience for help in returning her beloved children to her.

Similarly, Jeffrey Dahmer, early in his killing spree, appeared in court and lied so believably that he convinced a judge and jury that he had done nothing worse than drinking a little too much— when he had in fact already killed. This coolness, lack of guilt, and deception is the polar opposite of my patients' emotions—they feel dreadful pain and guilt for merely having bad thoughts and sometimes even confess to crimes they have not committed.

Simon, for example, had horrific thoughts that he would run over a pedestrian while driving. These thoughts caused him such intense guilt and shame that he rarely drove anymore. When he did venture out, simply driving over a pothole or a speed bump could trigger his bad thoughts. Sometimes they became so intense that he looked in his rearview mirror and actually "saw" the body of a pedestrian lying in the road. When this happened, he would turn his car around and repeatedly drive back to the spot, since he couldn't feel certain. He would then go home and listen to the television and radio news reports for the hit-and-run accident he was certain that he had committed. Once, his guilt became so intense that he finally gave up and telephoned the police to confess to a crime he had never committed.

Who Harms Babies?

Are there any predictors of which women will actually harm their children? In fact there are. A small percentage of women who suffer from postpartum depression develop a much more serious disorder called postpartum psychosis. Although I do not know any details about the case above of the woman charged with killing her baby in a microwave oven, my guess would be that she was suffering from a postpartum psychosis. Women suffering from postpartum psychosis lose touch with reality. As an example, one new mother "saw" yellow smoke coming from her infant's nostrils and ears and interpreted this as a sign that he was from the devil. She resolved that the only way to foil Satan was to leave her son in a trash can to die. Luckily her husband returned from work early, heard crying from the trash can, and saved the boy's life. The mother was then hospitalized, and her postpartum psychosis was successfully treated with medications and she returned to normal.

When Bad Thoughts Are Dangerous

Below are situations in which you should be concerned about your bad thoughts and seek professional treatment as soon as possible. Thankfully such circumstances are present in only a small minority of people suffering from bad thoughts.

If you do not feel upset by the thoughts but instead find them pleasurable.

Earlier I described a man who watched presidential speeches and papal audiences while planning where to stand to get a good shot at the speaker. He described these thoughts to me as mildly enjoyable and did not describe any guilt or disgust at having these thoughts. If, like him, you do not feel guilt or distress due to your bad thoughts, you should talk to a mental health professional about your thoughts to make sure that you won't one day act on them.

If you have ever acted on violent or sexual thoughts or urges in the past—either while sober or under the influence of alcohol or drugs.

I have seen several patients who, under the influence of alcohol or other drugs, acted violently or sexually in ways that got them into trouble with the law. When these individuals suffer with bad thoughts, it is extremely important that they get treatment to help them abstain from these substances that put them at high risk of acting on their thoughts and impulses. Remember that the best predictor of future behavior is past behavior. So if you look back on your life and see that you have acted in violent or sexually inappropriate ways toward animals or people, then you should take your bad thoughts seriously. It may be that you're not able to properly inhibit your urges as most people can (this is called an impulse control disorder), and you need treatment to learn how to do this.

If you hear voices, think people are against you, or see things that others do not see.

As you saw in the example of the new mother suffering from postpartum psychosis, hallucinations can be dangerous because they do not permit you to perceive reality accurately. If this is happening to you, please contact a mental health professional as soon as possible, because new medications are available that can rapidly treat these problems with only mild side effects.

If you feel uncontrollable anger and find it hard to resist urges to act on your aggressive impulses.

The students who fired on their classmates at Columbine High School were examples of this problem. If you feel extreme anger toward a particular person or group of people, please talk to a mental health professional—effective anger-management treatments exist to help you.

I end by emphasizing once again that the *vast majority* of people with bad thoughts will never act on their thoughts.

4

What Causes Bad Thoughts?

Truth in science can be defined as the working hypothesis best
suited to open the way to the next better one.
—Konrad Lorenz (1903–1989)

While no one knows precisely why we have bad thoughts, several
theories have been proposed—although for me, none eclipses the
elegance of Poe's Imp of the Perverse. These theories are not mu-
tually exclusive, but rather have large areas of overlap. No one
theory provides a complete explanation of bad thoughts. Because,
as far as we can tell, bad thoughts have appeared in all cultures,
and at all times in history, it seems a safe guess that these thoughts
are hardwired into our genetic makeup. This brings us to the evolutionary explanation of why we all have bad thoughts from time
to time.

What Causes Universal Bad Thoughts?

Evolutionary Theories

From the evolutionary viewpoint, the tendency to have sexual
and violent thoughts and urges (as well as to engage in these behaviors at appropriate times) has been bred into humans over
thousands of centuries, shaping our bodies and minds to help us

survive and reproduce. As an example, evolutionary theory predicts that the genes of our ancestors who *rarely thought* about sexual intercourse would gradually have become outnumbered by the genes of those who thought about sex quite a bit, and who—the theory would predict—produced more offspring as a result.

Evolutionary theory has proposed a similar explanation as to why human males tend to have more aggressive thoughts and to act more aggressively than females. Our male ancestors who thought and behaved most aggressively would have tended to become the leaders of their groups and, as a result, would have impregnated the most females, thus passing on their genes in larger numbers than did more docile males.

Similar controversial evolutionary explanations have been put forth to explain rape[1] and infanticide,[2] which both have important influences on selecting which males' genes win the evolutionary lottery by being passed down through the generations. In the case of forcible sexual attacks, evolutionary theory predicts that our male ancestors who raped, by impregnating some of their victims, might have passed along genes to their offspring resulting in a predisposition to rape. In the case of infanticide, studies in the United States and Canada have indeed confirmed the chilling fact that stepparents, who have no genetic investment in the children they must provide for, are far more likely to kill their stepchildren than are biological parents[3] (which, perhaps, explains the multitude of "wicked stepparents" in the ancient fairy tales that we still tell our children). The evolutionary explanation for this apparently senseless killing is that our male ancestors allocated their precious food and other resources only to their own biological children, rather than providing for the survival of the offspring of their male competitors, and hence their genes. Similar phenomena have been observed in other primate species. Indeed, at least one author has heard in Susan Smith's drowning of her two children echoes of these ancient evolutionary influences: "Her case is typical. Pregnant at nineteen and married in haste, Smith was estranged at twenty-three. . . . Unable, despite child support, to meet her debts, and spurned by a well-to-do lover who was unwilling to accept her children."[4]

The evolutionary viewpoint has also been applied to understanding why new mothers might worry about harming their newborn babies. In her paper on violent thoughts in postpartum depression described above, Dr. Katherine Wisner noted that *the more these mothers had violent thoughts about terrible things happening to their infants, the more they also checked their infants to ensure that they were safe.* This finding suggested to Dr. Wisner that perhaps these thoughts were selected by evolution in part because they made new mothers more vigilant to the very real dangers that could befall their children, thereby increasing their children's chances of survival, and hence passing along their "vigilance" genes.

Dr. Wisner believes that the evolutionary hypothesis of new mothers' obsessions about harming their infants is tenable. That is, it is possible that in humanity's early evolutionary history, those mothers who were extravigilant about their newborns—perhaps because of a brain chemistry biased toward obsessional thoughts about possible dangers to their babies and more checking on their safety—increased the chances of their offspring surviving to maturity and passing their genes down to future generations. Although the evolutionary hypothesis is speculative, Dr. Wisner is confident that, regardless of how they came to be, these terrible violent and sexual obsessions are related in some way to the brain chemistry of mothering, which appears to have gone astray in some women.[5]

The aggressive and sexual impulses that evolutionary theory predicts were bred into us are thought to be controlled by "lower parts" of our brains—that is, those parts we share with other mammals. On a more optimistic side, this viewpoint explains that as humans came together into communities, their brains developed structures to keep raw sexual and violent thoughts and urges under control—that is, to "inhibit" them. The main role of our species' large orbital-frontal cortex (the part of the brain that rests above the orbits of our eyes—hence the name *orbital*—and behind our large, and no-longer back-sloping, forehead) is to determine whether to act on the thoughts and impulses generated in the lower parts of our brains, or as is the case most of the time, to inhibit acting on them. Evolutionary theory suggests that through this process we come into contact with the violent and sexual instincts that have been passed down to us over the millennia.

To wrap up this brief overview of the evolutionary theory of bad thoughts, I would add my own theory that my patients' problems with bad thoughts arise when either (1) they cannot accept that such urges and thoughts are part of being human, or (2) they fear that their orbital-frontal cortex will not be able to inhibit these thoughts and urges. As an example of the first case, Isaac—the man who worried he wanted to have sex with animals—was unable to progress until he came to see his thoughts as the random bad thoughts that pass through everyone's mind from time to time, rather than as proof that he was a pervert who did not deserve to live in human society. Thus, he recognized that the bad thoughts per se were not his biggest problem, but rather his overly strict reaction to his thoughts. Kay, who fears stabbing her sleeping children, is an example of the second case—she remains stuck and unwilling to undertake treatment because she still believes that she will one day act on her urges; until she has faith that, despite her fears, her brain will not let her do this, she will make little progress.

Freud and the Imp of the Perverse

An apparent paradox arises from the evolutionary viewpoint. As explained above, evolutionary theory says that our orbital-frontal cortex grew larger, at least in part, to inhibit sexual and violent behaviors that would be detrimental to the individual's ability to live in society. As a result, it is difficult to explain why *opposite* evolutionary pressures should have existed for our ancestors to engage in *socially inappropriate behavior*. Why do we, for example, sometimes think about doing the most inappropriate thing at the most inappropriate time—as with blasphemous thoughts in church?

Perhaps the problem cannot be viewed wholly from the evolutionary perspective. Sigmund Freud approached this question in his classic book *Totem and Taboo* by reminding us that taboos would be unnecessary if people did not *desire* to do things that could be detrimental to society. For example, commandments such as "Thou shalt not kill" or "Thou shalt not commit adultery" would be unnecessary if these things never happened.

Freud emphasizes the conflict we are sure to feel when our sexual and violent thoughts and urges (biological remnants of our evolutionary past, which he called the id) clash head-on with newer, tighter restrictions in a carefully regulated society such as that of his Victorian era. Freud also theorized that through socialization, we internalize the social prohibitions of our culture in what he called the superego (some readers may see a strong similarity between the functions of the orbital-frontal cortex described above and Freud's superego).

At the risk of putting words in Freud's mouth, we could say that the Imp of the Perverse was born from this social versus biological clash; that is, the tension between our inbred sexual and violent impulses and society's strictures against our freely engaging in these behaviors. In other writings, Freud showed that humor developed in part as a safe and socially approved way of dissipating this tension—think about ever-popular sexual and bathroom humor, and "innocent" aggressive jokes poking fun at others.

Thought Suppression and Bad Thoughts

As interesting as evolutionary and Freudian theories are, both are ultimately untestable. They are useful mainly as aids to our thinking about how these bad thoughts may have come about. A more recent theory, called thought suppression, proposed by Dr. Daniel Wegner, has the advantage of being testable by experiment and also suggests a treatment approach to reduce bad thoughts.

In the original preface to his superb book *White Bears and Other Unwanted Thoughts*, Dr. Wegner explains how he chose his title:

You would think this book was about white bears, given the title and all. And in a way, it is. Although the topic is really unwanted thoughts and how people try to control them, white bears come into the picture because of a story about the young Tolstoy. It seems he was once challenged by his older brother to stand in a corner until he could stop thinking of a white bear. Of course he stood there confused for some time. And the point was made: We do not seem to have much control over our minds, especially when it comes to suppressing thoughts that are unwanted.[6]

Oversimplified, Wegner's theory states that anytime we try to force ourselves *not* to think a particular thought, the thought is paradoxically given more energy. Further, not only are we unable to suppress the thought, but our attempt backfires by producing a rebound effect in which the thought occurs *more* frequently after we finally stop trying to suppress it, that is, to give up actively trying to force ourselves to not think a particular thought.

As Freud pointed out, society strongly discourages sexual and violent thoughts that could be socially disruptive. Wegner would argue that, because of such societal taboos, taught in the home and church, we learn to vigilantly monitor our thoughts—and whenever we detect an inappropriate thought, we try instantly to suppress it. But, as Wegner points out, by so doing, we are our own worst enemy—in reality we are beginning an endless cycle of failed thought suppression, a rebounding of more intense thoughts, and then another unsuccessful attempt at thought suppression.

Wegner's theory has given us a tool to use in treating our patients with bad thoughts. The turning point to recovery for some patients can be telling them that it is perfectly normal to have bad thoughts from time to time, and that trying to suppress these thoughts is what can turn them into problems. By stopping thought suppression, as did the priest described in an earlier chapter, and letting the thoughts pass normally through the mind, the thoughts are less bothersome and are less noticed.

On the other hand, though thought suppression certainly plays a role in the kind of normal bad thoughts I have been describing, I do not agree that it is decisive in the development of clinical obsessions. For, even though nearly everyone engages in some thought suppression for their unpleasant thoughts, only a minority are tormented or paralyzed by their obsessions. So what causes normal bad thoughts to progress from merely annoying to painful and debilitating?

Why Do Bad Thoughts Get out of Control?

Research suggests that a psychiatric disorder such as depression, OCD, obsessive-compulsive personality disorder, Tourette's syndrome, or post–traumatic stress disorder is almost always present in those people suffering from clinically severe bad thoughts.

Depression

As I described earlier, mothers suffering from depression, whether immediately following the birth of a child or later on, are at higher risk of having violent thoughts about their children than are mothers who are not depressed. For example, Dr. Jennings and associates in Pittsburgh interviewed one hundred clinically depressed mothers with a child under three years of age and found that forty-one percent admitted to having violent thoughts about harming their child, compared to only seven percent of forty-six undepressed mothers.[7]

Being depressed forces us to look at ourselves and our world through dark-colored glasses, and it predisposes us to having more bad thoughts about death and danger. Along these same lines, a group of researchers in England recently reported on four women treated for their pathological fear of "cot death" (usually referred to as sudden infant death syndrome, or SIDS, in the United States).[8] All these women were depressed, and all excessively checked their baby's breathing during the night.

Characteristics of clinical depression are listed below in table 6. As you can see from the final characteristic, when depressed we often think the worst of ourselves.[9] This often leads us to experience normal bad thoughts as evidence that we are worthless, sinful, bad people who are deserving of punishment.

TABLE 6
CHARACTERISTICS OF CLINICAL DEPRESSION

- feeling blue, sad, empty, or tearful most of the time
- loss of interest or pleasure in most activities that used to be enjoyable
- decreased appetite and weight loss, or increased appetite and weight gain
- trouble sleeping or sleeping too much
- feeling slowed down most of the time or feeling very restless most of the time
- feeling very tired and without energy most of the time
- trouble thinking, concentrating, or making decisions most of the time
- thinking about death or suicide a lot
- decreased interest in sex
- feeling worthless or guilty about past mistakes

Modified from American Psychiatric Association, *Diagnostic and Statistical Manual of Mental Disorders*, 4th ed. (Washington, D.C.: American Psychiatric Association, 1994).

It is especially important to make a clear distinction between the bad thoughts that are the subject of this book, and the suicidal thoughts that are common in depression. If you have frequent and strong thoughts like

- fantasizing about how you would kill yourself
- images of yourself lying in a coffin
- strong impulses to cut yourself
- strong impulses to shoot yourself with a gun
- strong impulses to take an overdose of pills
- strong impulses to hang yourself
- strong impulses to jump out of a window
- strong impulses to crash your automobile
- images or fantasies about doing any of these things

then you should take these thoughts or impulses seriously and talk to a mental health professional about them as soon as possible. These thoughts *can be* dangerous and are different from the type of harmless sexual, aggressive, and religious bad thoughts that are the subject of this book.

Tourette's Syndrome

Tourette's syndrome is a neuropsychiatric disorder that illustrates the tension between our sexual and aggressive impulses and society's taboos. In no other disorder is the Imp of the Perverse as clearly at work! For here, besides the muscle tics and twitches, and the odd sounds that are the cardinal signs of this disorder, sufferers sometimes shout the rudest obscenities in public, may engage in masturbatory motions, and frequently complain of sexual and violent thoughts and urges.

Here is one of the earliest recorded accounts of Tourette's syndrome:

> In the mid–fifteenth century a worried father and his son traveled from Central Europe to Rome to seek the advice of an exorcist. Until recently, the father explained, his son had enjoyed a well-earned reputation as a talented preacher of the gospel. To the man's horror, however, his son had recently developed strange and uncontrollable urges to grimace and curse whenever he found himself in a church. The son, too, was justly frightened, living as he did at a time when presumed witches were summarily executed. When asked to explain his behavior, the young man said he felt as if a demon had taken control of his will. "I cannot help myself at all," he said, "for so he uses all my limbs and organs . . . causing me to speak or to cry out; and I hear the words as if they were spoken by myself, but I am altogether unable to restrain them." Fearing satanic possession, the father had decided that the only hope was to drive out the infecting demon.[10]

Anything that a Touretter is told *not* to do can instantly become the aim of an insistent urge. Patients have told me that they have felt compelled to shove knives into electric outlets, to shift their car into reverse while driving at high speed, to pluck out their eyeball, to pull fire alarms, to touch other people on the nose, and to shout racial slurs or blasphemies in church. And unlike sufferers of OCD, every one of these patients has acted on these urges many times!

Neurologist Oliver Sacks has given us several case studies of Touretters that beautifully illustrate the psychological complexity of the disorder. Recently, he wrote of a visit with a Canadian surgeon with Tourette's, showing the Imp of the Perverse at play in this amazing man. In these two different scenarios, whatever behavior was most prohibited at that particular moment was instantly seized upon by the imp:

> The next patient was a heavy woman with a melanoma on her buttock, which needed to be excised at some depth. Bennett scrubbed up, donned sterile gloves. Something about the sterile field, the prohibition, seemed to stir his Tourette's; he made sudden darting motions, or incipient motions, of his sterile, gloved right hand toward the ungloved, unwashed, "dirty" part of his left arm. The patient eyed this without expression.[11]

And again:

> Bennett preparing for the operating room was a startling sight. "You should scrub next to him," his young assistant said. "It's quite an experience." It was indeed, for what I saw in the outpatient clinic was magnified here: constant sudden dartings and reachings with the hands, almost but never quite touching the unscrubbed, unsterile shoulder, his assistant, the mirror; sudden lungings, and touchings of his colleagues with his feet; and a barrage of vocalizations— "Hooty-hooo! Hooty-hooo!"—suggestive of a huge owl.[12]

Like the surgeon described by Dr. Sacks, many of my patients with Tourette's syndrome have felt tempted to do the most inappropriate thing at the most inappropriate time. For a surgeon this might be making sterilized hands dirty, but for my patient, Brad, a traveling salesman in his early forties who spent most of his time driving, his urges focused on ruining his automobile. Although the drug Haldol had controlled most of his many tics, twitches, and grunts, when Brad first came to see me, he described being left with occasional urges to do dangerous things, such as throw his car into reverse gear at 55 mph on the highway! (As he told me this, I recalled having wondered what would happen if I did such a thing—the Imp of the Perverse is never far.) Brad explained to me that when the urge struck, he had enough control to delay it until he had safely pulled into the breakdown lane, slowed down, and made sure no cars were behind him. Then, wham! He jammed the automatic gearshift forward from D to R and felt the gears grind as the gearbox locked up and was ruined, and the car finally jolted to a stop. "Oh, yes," Brad added as he told me of a key precaution he takes as a result of his urge, "I only drive rental cars."

OCD and Tourette's syndrome are believed to be genetically linked and also to share neurological pathways. Interestingly, several recent studies have found that sufferers of OCD are far *less* likely to suffer from violent or sexual obsessions unless they *also* suffer from the tics and twitches of Tourette's syndrome. For example, Dr. Leckman and his associates at Yale University found that patients with tic-related OCD reported more aggressive, religious, and sexual obsessions than patients with OCD but with no tics.[13] Similarly, Dr. Zohar and his associates at Hebrew University in Israel studied adolescents suffering from OCD and found that those with tics were more prone to aggressive and sexual images and obsessions than those without tics (and that these differences could not be explained by the gender of the child).[14]

Table 7 lists the characteristics of Tourette's syndrome.

TABLE 7
CHARACTERISTICS OF TOURETTE'S SYNDROME

- Before age 18, had several muscle tics and at least one vocal tic (sound or noise)
- The tics happened many times a day for more than a year, and child was never without all tics for more than three months in a row

Examples of Muscle Tics
- *Face*
  • winking, rolling eyes, curling in eyelids, staring, raising eyebrows, scalp movements, frowning, wrinkling nose, twitching nostrils, flaring nostrils, opening mouth, grimacing, snarling, pouting, pursing lips, twitching lips, spitting, flicking tongue, nibbling, licking, gnawing, grinding teeth, biting inside of cheek, protruding jaw, sucking, rubbing chin
- *Head or Neck*
  • tossing head, nodding head, jerking head, drooping head, rolling head, swiveling head, shrugging shoulders, hunching shoulders, stretching neck
- *Arms*
  • jerking arms, clenching fists, stretching fingers, flicking arms, piano-playing movements, straightening arms, bending arms, stretching shoulders backwards
- *Body*
  • thrusting pelvis, jerking abdomen, twitching chest, protruding abdomen, tightening buttocks, expanding chest, tightening sphincter, shudders
- *Legs*
  • shaking foot and toes, flexing hips, kicking, curling toes, stretching foot, extending knee, bending knees

Examples of Vocal Tics
  throat clearing
  barking
  sniffing
  snorting
  grunting
  cursing
  repeating words of others
  gulping
  squeaking
  shrieking
  hiccuping
  clicking
  raspberry noises

gasping	saying "yahoo"
deep breathing	quacking
belching	saying "ha, ha, ha"
hooting	panting
humming	repeating sounds like: Sh,
hissing	Sh, Sh, T, T, T, T, Ooh,
sucking noise	Ugh
growling	

Modified from American Psychiatric Association, *Diagnostic and Statistical Manual of Mental Disorders*, 4th ed. (Washington, D.C.: American Psychiatric Association, 1994), and from A. J. Lees: *Tics and Related Disorders.* Edinburgh: Churchill Livingstone, 1985.

Obsessive-Compulsive Personality Disorder

Many individuals who suffer from bad thoughts would also be diagnosed with obsessive-compulsive personality disorder (OCPD). The criteria for this disorder are listed on page 41. As you can see by the first characteristic, these people tend to be inflexible and perfectionistic about moral or religious matters. For them, it is unforgivable to experience even a single bad thought, even if they acknowledge that other people have them as well. Especially if this person's view of religion includes a vengeful, punitive God, he or she will have little tolerance for any normal bad thoughts that pass through his or her mind (which might barely be noticed by another person).

In earlier times, individuals with OCPD were considered to have "sensitive consciences"—which, come to think of it, probably better described their problem and vulnerability than today's modern acronym.

Obsessive-Compulsive Disorder

OCD sufferers either have intrusive thoughts that they can't get out of their mind or perform rituals over and over, or both. (The diagnostic criteria for OCD are listed on page 36).

My colleagues Drs. Cary Savage and Scott Rauch, and our research team at the Massachusetts General Hospital/Harvard Medical School, found recently that sufferers of OCD are often unable to pay adequate attention to events they are not actively focusing upon. As a result these events are not stored in their memories, as happens automatically for most of us. As an example, although I cannot actually picture locking my car door this morning, some automatic part of my brain was functioning then and registered that I did this. This is called implicit learning, because I wasn't actively, or explicitly, focusing on locking the door at the time. Yet, I have a gut feeling of certainty that I did it, even though I can't actually picture doing it. This is probably the reason that patients with OCD stare at a light switch for many minutes, yet still feel that it "doesn't register in their mind that the switch is off."

By the same token, OCD sufferers often cannot feel certain that they have not performed an inappropriate action they have thought about *because they cannot remember not having done it!* Although I can't specifically remember *not* having sexually molested anyone on the street earlier today, my brain was properly monitoring my actions and automatically gathered the information to give me the safe gut feeling that I did nothing wrong. On the other hand, consider my patient who worries that he will unknowingly have sex with passersby on the street. When later he tries to feel certain he has *not* molested or been molested, he searches his memory for proof—but, not finding it, he becomes even more afraid, since, being overconscientious (and wanting absolute certainty), he draws the erroneous conclusion that because he can't remember *not* having done it, he *must have* sexually molested someone. (You'll see later that learning how to identify and correct such irrational beliefs is at the heart of a new treatment for bad thoughts called cognitive therapy.)

Much of our research in the last decade has been aimed at understanding what goes on in the brains of OCD sufferers causing their intrusive thoughts and compulsions. By using new brain-scanning technologies, along with careful assessment with neuropsychological tests of attention and memory, our research team has begun to piece together a comprehensive picture of this mysterious disorder.

For the first time in history, we are now able to actually see what happens in the brains of people while they are having bad thoughts. Dr. Savage explains that our studies using brain imaging show that when our patients have intrusive obsessions, specific parts of their brains become more active: these include the orbital-frontal cortex, the caudate nucleus, and the anterior cingulum, all of which are closely connected with our limbic system, the part of the brain involved with strong feelings. This explains why people usually obsess about things that involve danger of harm or humiliation.

To demonstrate, Dr. Savage gives the example of a woman afraid of knives. If, despite her efforts to avoid them, she sees a knife, this activates her brain's limbic system and she becomes aware of feeling scared. Then, if due to OCD, the parts of the brain described above, despite working overtime, are not able to completely suppress this feeling and keep it from her awareness, then she will probably suffer from obsessions and worries about the knife and the damage it can do.

Recall my patient Kay, the mother who spent hours worrying that she would stab her boy and girl while they lay sleeping. How would a neuropsychologist such as Dr. Savage try to reassure Kay that she *will not* act on obsessions like stabbing her children? He might tell her, "Although you worry that your brain is not able to inhibit your acting on your thoughts and urges, our brain scans show that, in reality, the proper parts of your brain—such as your orbital-frontal cortex—are actually working extrahard and succeeding in inhibiting your urges. In fact, your brain activity is the *exact opposite* of that of a person who acts impulsively and dangerously. In the very same areas that your brain is working extrahard, their brains are underactive." In the end, Dr. Savage would try to help Kay see that she is wasting her time worrying and trying to inhibit her thoughts and impulses because the correct parts of her brain are already automatically doing this job for her.

How are OCD and Tourette's syndrome related in the brain? Dr. Savage recommends that we think of these two disorders as lying upon a continuum, with the particular symptoms we see determined by which brain systems are malfunctioning. He cites Tourette's syndrome, in which the brain's motor networks (that is, nerves that are connected to various muscles) are primarily affected. As a result, we see a variety of muscular tics, twitches, and jerks, along with sounds produced by the vocal musculature. In OCD, on the other hand, Dr. Savage believes that prefrontal cognitive networks involved in thinking are probably affected, so we see more mental symptoms such as obsessive thoughts and worries.

But why do sufferers of Tourette's syndrome say the most inappropriate thing at the most inappropriate time? As an example, Lowell Handler, a sufferer of this disorder, writes in his recent book *Twitch and Shout*[15] about an acquaintance of his who had Tourette's syndrome and was a lesbian: "She lived with her parents and was most afraid of them discovering her sexual preference. The one word she blurted out time and time again, loudly, and often, was gay. Here is the Imp of the Perverse at his best; but what happens in the brain to produce this? Dr. Savage believes that the urges to say or do these things are tightly tied into the limbic, or emotional, system of the brain because these acts are all dangerous, provocative, or shocking. That, he explains, is why it is no accident that the words shouted out tend to be those the sufferer might feel most ashamed to shout out.

All of us have witnessed friends who drink too much alcohol and then act inappropriately, perhaps doing some of the embarrassing or dangerous things that OCD sufferers fear doing. Why is this? What is happening in the brain to cause this? Dr. Savage explains that alcohol and or recreational drugs such as barbiturates suppress the activity of our brain's frontal cortex, whose main job is to control and suppress the primitive aggressive and sexual impulses from the lower areas of our brain. When we drink or use drugs, our frontal cortex is no longer able to do its job properly, making us more likely to act on our impulses. Because of this, for anyone who worries about doing something dangerous or embarrassing—such as someone with OCD—getting intoxicated with any substance is usually a bad idea. Several of my patients with OCD have told me about times when they have drunk too much, blacked out, and the next morning were tormented trying to remember whether they had done something inappropriate— from sexually molesting someone in the house to having urinated in the orange juice! They unanimously agreed that the terrible fear they felt the next morning—worse than any hangover—far outweighed the temporary high they had felt the night before.

Earlier, you met Gary, a father obsessed with possibly having sexually molested his young daughter or her friend. Try as he might to feel certain, he said he simply couldn't remember *not* having done something wrong, which kept his fear going. What could be happening in his brain to keep him caught in this awful negative loop? Dr. Savage explains that we see the symptoms of OCD only when *both* (1) emotional systems of the limbic system and (2) cognitive systems of the prefrontal cortex are malfunctioning. When these two problems coexist, OCD sufferers such as Gary will place tremendous emotional importance on their thoughts and worry about them excessively. To make matters worse, these two problems are related to yet other problems Gary's brain has in processing a particular kind of memory called episodic memory. Episodic memory is your ability to re-create past events in your head. When you add all these problems together, you can see why Gary feels anxious and worries that he has done something wrong in the past but can't remember it—all in all, a terribly upsetting feeling. Dr. Savage gives an analogy: "Although I can't remember whether I locked the door to my house this morning, this worry doesn't have a lot of importance to me, because it doesn't activate my limbic system in the same way as it would someone with OCD—because they are excessively concerned with safety and worries about making a mistake and being blamed for it."

Some of my patients describe vivid images they have as part of their bad thoughts. They tell me that when they are worried about something happening, they can at times actually "see" it happen. For example, if they fear hitting someone while driving, they might look in the rearview mirror and "see" a body lying behind them in the road. One patient of mine described vivid images of animals run over on the road; another "saw" body parts strewn around as if on a battlefield. Such strong images make bad thoughts even more upsetting than less visual obsessions. What can be happening in these people's brain to produce these strange experiences? Dr. Savage notes that although patients with OCD are clearly not schizophrenic, what some experience *is like* a hallucination. My colleague at Harvard Dr. Stephen Kosslyn has performed many studies of visual imagery proving that when I form an image in my mind of some event, I am *activating exactly the same areas of my brain* that I would have were I actually seeing the event. As a result, Dr. Savage speculates that OCD sufferers like Gary may be reestablishing their feared images frequently, and by doing so it may eventually become hard for them to differentiate what they are imagining from what they are actually seeing. By the same token, an OCD sufferer such as Gary who checks his memory over and over again may actually harm his memory of the things he did and didn't do, as it becomes more difficult for him to differentiate one episode from another.

As an interested onlooker of the neuroscience scene, I am at times struck by the similarities between the results of our imaging studies and some of Freud's early ideas about the superego's trying to inhibit primitive impulses from rising up from the ancient id. To the extent that neuroscience's orbital-frontal cortex does a lot of the same things that Freud hypothesized the superego would do, Dr. Savage agrees that neuroscience's limbic system is suspiciously similar to Freud's id. In fact, Freud hypothesized that the superego was overactive in OCD—I bet he'd love to see our brain scan images showing the orbital-frontal cortex lit bright red in overactivity in OCD. Perhaps the old saying is true, and there really is nothing new under the sun.

Post–Traumatic Stress Disorder

Post–traumatic stress disorder (PTSD) is characterized by recurrent memories, flashbacks, and nightmares of some traumatic event. The key difference from OCD is that sufferers of PTSD suffer from memories of *actual traumatic events* that have happened to them—in OCD the sufferer thinks about imagined catastrophes that might occur. Table 8 lists the characteristics of this disorder.

TABLE 8
CHARACTERISTICS OF POST–TRAUMATIC STRESS DISORDER (PTSD)

- Person was exposed to a traumatic event
  • either witnessed or experienced an event that involved or threatened injury or death
  • felt intense fear, helplessness, or horror at the time
- Person still re-experiences the event
  • Still has frequent and intrusive memories of the event (images, thoughts, feelings)
  • Still has frequent, distressing dreams of the event
  • Feels as if the traumatic event is happening again
  • Feels strong distress and fear when confronted with things that remind her of the event
- Person still avoids things associated with the trauma
  • Avoids thoughts, feelings, or conversations about the trauma
  • Avoids activities, places, or people that remind her of the trauma
  • Not able to remember important parts of the trauma
- Person still often feels numb
  • Less interested in activities that used to be enjoyable
  • Feels detached or disconnected from other people
  • Unable to have loving or angry feelings
  • Does not expect to have a career, marriage, children, or long life
- Person often feels anxious or afraid
  • Trouble falling or staying asleep
  • Often irritable or angry
  • Trouble concentrating
  • Feeling always on guard
  • "Jumpy" in response to loud or sudden noises

Modified from American Psychiatric Association, *Diagnostic and Statistical Manual of Mental Disorders,* 4th ed. (Washington, D.C.: American Psychiatric Association, 1994).

It is important to distinguish intrusive bad thoughts about violence, sex, or blasphemy from images or memories of past traumatic experiences. This is especially important when the trauma has been severe, and the resulting psychological problems are severe and require professional help. In her classic book, *Trauma and Recovery: The Aftermath of Violence—from Domestic Abuse to Political Terror,* Dr. Judith Herman discusses her patients who suffer from what she calls complex PTSD, including those who have experienced:

> A history of subjection to totalitarian control over a prolonged period (months to years). Examples include hostages, prisoners of war, concentration camp survivors, and survivors of religious cults. Examples often include those subjected to totalitarian systems in sexual and domestic life, including survivors of domestic battering, childhood physical or sexual abuse, and organized sexual exploitation.[16]

Individuals exposed to such traumatic situations often experience the following symptoms, which are different from the harmless violent, sexual, and blasphemous thoughts that are the subject of this book:

- frequent thoughts of suicide
- frequent thoughts of harming themselves
- reliving past experiences over and over again
- strong fear of feeling or expressing any angry feelings
- extremely inhibited anger
- images of violence toward the abuser
- strong fear or disgust with sex
- upsetting images about sex

Dr. Herman explained the characteristics of the traumatic memory this way:

> The traumatic moment becomes encoded in an abnormal form of memory, which breaks spontaneously into consciousness, both as flashbacks during waking states and as traumatic nightmares during sleep. Small, seemingly insignificant reminders can also evoke these memories, which often return with all the vividness and emotional force of the original event. Thus even normally safe environments may come to feel dangerous, for the survivor can never be

assured that she will not encounter some reminder of the trauma.[17]

There are effective treatments for PTSD and for complex PTSD, many of which are described in Dr. Herman's outstanding book. If you think you may be suffering from this disorder, I suggest you first read as much as you can about it, then talk to a mental health professional you feel you can trust.

CASE EXAMPLE: OVERLAP OF BAD THOUGHTS AND PTSD

The intricate and sometimes confusing relationship between bad thoughts and PTSD was brought home to me by Janie when she first came to see me. Janie, a young professional woman, struck me at first as exceedingly shy. Although she was polite and at times looked *toward* me, she never seemed to look *at* me. Not until our second visit did I feel comfortable enough with Janie to ask her why she never seemed to make eye contact with me.

By that time, she had admitted to me, reluctantly, that she was tormented by violent and sexual thoughts toward coworkers, and in many other situations, too, such as in crowded buses or trains. Knowing that Janie—like most of my other patients—was exquisitely sensitive about her bad thoughts, I asked her carefully, "Do you not make eye contact with me because doing this might trigger you to have bad thoughts about *me*?" Janie, now looking down at the floor, nodded. "That's part of it," she added after a few beats. When she didn't expand on this after a few seconds of silence, I asked what other reason she might have.

Again Janie paused. Still looking at the linoleum floor of my office, she added, "If you look in my eyes, you'll see in them the awful things I've done." Janie explained that she was also occasionally troubled by thoughts—which she worried might be true memories—of having been sexually abused when she was a little girl.

Here was my first clue of a complicated relationship for Janie between PTSD and obsessive bad thoughts. This relationship became clearer to me when I helped Janie write out an exposure script for her bad thoughts about molesting children.[18] When Janie recorded this script, with my assistance, in her own voice on a loop tape and listened to it the next night, she paged me to tell me that something odd had happened.

After listening for a while to the loop tape, in which she was acting on her worst fears of molesting a young child in a shower, she told me that anxiety had begun to mount, and then she went numb, feeling dissociated from her surroundings. Then she began experiencing a flashback memory of *herself* as the young child being molested in the shower. During this experience—which is common in flashbacks of PTSD—Janie told me that she had *felt* physical memories of the molestation, just as if it were happening right then.

This was another warning signal to me—and I told Janie that this suggested that we might also have to proceed slowly with exposure therapy for these PTSD "memories" as well. (Like many of my patients, Janie then began to obsess and feel guilty about whether she could be *absolutely certain* that these events had occurred. I told her that since she was having "sense memories," we should agree to a working hypothesis for now that these memories *were* true, so she wouldn't have to obsess over that.

At one of our next sessions, the overlap between her OCD and PTSD once again reared its head. As Janie was writing out a detailed exposure script for the blasphemous and violent thoughts that she suffered when she entered a church, she spoke of the intense anger she felt toward the Church in general, and the family priest in particular, for "not having encouraged me to talk about the abuse," thus indirectly enabling it to continue.

Janie's mind had apparently transformed her childhood anger toward the Church, which she had never been able to express directly, into violent thoughts toward others who had not directly harmed her. Sigmund Freud had termed such a phenomenon "displacement." When in Janie's case the gold-standard treatment of exposure therapy did not work correctly—that is, habituation did not occur[19]—I sought to diagnose the real problem, which led to an awareness of PTSD symptoms, and possibly an abuse history.

The weeks that followed Janie's first flashbacks were not peaceful. She paged me often telling me that she felt terribly guilty, and at times suicidal, for thinking that such terrible things had happened. This is a common experience in severe PTSD and is an important reason why a trained mental health professional should treat this combination of problems.

Janie's OCD symptoms rapidly decreased—and she is now dealing with her flashback memories of abuse and worries about whether the events actually occurred. Through recounting these memories—with careful description of physical memories, such as feeling held down, nausea, and choking—she is gradually coming to terms with these other problems. It is hard work that will take time, but Janie is committed to seeing it through.

For patients whose bad thoughts do not respond to the standard behavioral or medication treatments, I now routinely ask them about past traumatic experiences. In a number of cases they have then recalled physical, emotional, or sexual abuse that has not been adequately dealt with. Although we are still researching this area, and our results are not conclusive, we are optimistic that after treatment for their PTSD, these individuals will be able to successfully tackle their bad thoughts.

Highly Sensitive People

Until recently, a piece seemed to me to be missing from these scientific explanations: Why do my patients worry so much about their thoughts? None of the theories described above seemed to answer this fundamental question.

In conducting support groups for people with bad thoughts, I tried to look for similarities between the participants, identifying characteristics that might help me better understand this problem. Finally, after about a year, a consistent pattern began to take shape. With only one or two exceptions, all of the participants said that, as children, they had been highly sensitive, especially in social situations but also to loud sounds and strong emotions. They were generally shy when young, were sensitive to being picked on by other children, and finally, had a hard time expressing anger toward others.

These observations led me to the medical school library to research the literature on "sensitive" people. My search first turned up a recent best-selling book for the general public entitled *The*

Highly Sensitive Person by Dr. Elaine Aron. That humans differ greatly in how reactive their nervous systems are to the same stimulation from the environment is well-documented. Dr. Aron focuses on those individuals, perhaps fifteen to twenty percent of all people, who are very sensitive to stimulation—those she calls "highly sensitive people" (or, as she refers to them, HSP). Dr. Aron has interviewed several hundred HSP to learn more about them, and how this sensitivity of their nervous system affects them positively and negatively. Two results of her surveys caught my eye: (1) HSP are "highly conscientious," and (2) they "are often thinking about their own thinking."[20] This was beginning to sound more and more like the patients in my group!

As I looked into this phenomenon further, I found references to it by the great Russian physiologist Ivan Pavlov (who used the terms *weak nervous system* and *neuroticism*), and also by Freud's Swiss disciple Carl Jung (who used the term *introversion* and described these people who are highly sensitive to their environment as being lost in the world of thoughts). My colleague at Harvard Dr. Jerome Kagan has spent the majority of his career carefully studying the development of this trait in children as young as four months old! As I reread *Galen's Prophecy*, Kagan's authoritative book on the subject, I came upon a quote that again seemed to perfectly describe my patients with bad thoughts:

> Anxiety and guilt over violations of moral standards are mediated by some of the same limbic circuits that mediate high reactivity and inhibition [this is a behavioral description of what we usually refer to as "shyness" and discomfort around new situations and especially strangers—LB]. Thus, inhibited children might be more susceptible to these moral emotions and biologically prepared to feel more intense guilt or anxiety over asocial behavior. If such children grow up in home environments that insist on obedience, they should show signs of unusually strict standards on the behaviors that their families regard as inappropriate.[21]

This hypothesis of a connection between suffering from bad thoughts and having been an inhibited or highly sensitive child has presented itself to me only recently and is yet to be scientifically tested. Yet, so far at least, the connections seem to me to fit and, more importantly, to make sense to many of my patients. For many of them, this discussion has enabled them to talk about how afraid they have been about feeling, let alone expressing, strong emotions such as fear, even since earliest childhood; how conscientious they have always been, and how this has led to strict thought suppression from an early age; how their obsessions can sometimes be triggered by imagined social slights that may seem insignificant to others; and perhaps most importantly, why they pay so much attention to, and place so much importance upon their thoughts.

By now you have some understanding of what causes bad thoughts—from evolutionary forces that shaped our ancestors' sexual and aggressive tendencies, to society's taboos against expression of these tendencies, to the problems caused by the usual practice of simply trying to suppress our bad thoughts, and finally to the coexisting psychiatric diagnoses that can lead to clinically severe bad thoughts that require treatment. Also, you should be able to recognize other thoughts and impulses that can be confused with harmless bad thoughts, but which should be taken seriously. Now it is time to consider the treatments that have proven effective for violent, sexual, and blasphemous bad thoughts.

PART TWO

TREATMENT OF BAD THOUGHTS

5

Facing Your Fears Head-on: Exposure Therapy

You gain strength, courage, and confidence by every experience in which you really stop to look fear in the face. You are able to say to yourself, "I lived through this horror. I can take the next thing that comes along."

—Anna Eleanor Roosevelt (1884–1962)

Many of my patients are shocked when I tell them that to overcome their bad thoughts they are going to have to face them head-on. "Isn't there an easier way?" they often ask, reminding me that they've done all they could for years to avoid thinking about these things. My answer is that we have yet to find a treatment that works as well and as rapidly as directly confronting or "exposing" yourself to the very thing that you fear. Indeed, extensive research around the world since the late 1960s on the use of this "exposure therapy" for OCD has confirmed that repeated exposures of one to two hours at a time are highly effective in reducing obsessions in most sufferers.

The principles of exposure therapy can be stated simply:

Expose yourself to the thing that most triggers your fear or discomfort for one to two hours at a time, without leaving the situation, or doing anything else to distract or comfort you.

Do not be misled, however, by the simplicity of these instructions, for they contain powerful medicine. For example, two recent neuro-imaging studies at UCLA proved that the following of these seemingly simple instructions is the first nondrug treatment to show changes in the brain chemistry of responders that mirror their observable clinical improvements. Similarly, my colleague Dr. Isaac Marks of the Maudsley Hospital in London has lectured around the world on the vital importance of spreading comparatively simple medical information as widely as possible. In a wonderful analogy he reminds us that, despite all the millions of dollars spent on high-tech medical and imaging equipment, the following simple instructions dispersed by the World Health Organization (WHO) to mothers in third world countries have saved many more lives:

> The instruction is for the mother to boil a cup of water, put into it a pinch of salt lifted with three (not two or four) fingers, stir it, taste it, and if it's no saltier than tears and not too hot, to spoon it to her baby, who is likely to absorb it without vomiting.

Behind that simple instruction, Professor Marks reminds us, are two hundred years of Western scientific endeavor concerning the nature of dehydration and blood osmolarity and how to correct it. With that instruction one can do away with the need for intravenous fluid and all the paraphernalia it entails. Mums can treat their babies in the bush.

The simple rules of exposure therapy are similar to the WHO instructions in that both are behavioral instructions, and both rely on the individual's accepting the advice as worthwhile, nondangerous, and effective.

Habituation: The Key to Exposure Therapy

To understand why exposure therapy is so effective, it is important first to understand the key principle upon which it is based: habituation. Patients have told me they appreciate the way

I describe habituation in my book about treating OCD, *Getting Control*:

Have you ever visited friends who live near an airport or train station? You've probably wondered how in the world they can stand the noise. But your friends seem hardly to notice it. Or have you ever squeezed into a painfully tight pair of shoes in the morning, only to find that by evening you've forgotten you have them on? If you've had either of these experiences, you've witnessed your body's process of habituation firsthand. *Habituation*, which comes from the Latin word *habitus*, for "habit," means "to accustom; to make familiar by frequent use or practice." In other words, after long familiarity with a situation that at first produces a strong emotional reaction, our bodies learn to get used to or ignore that situation.

Habituation is a key process to understand if you want to control your compulsions and obsessions. Our research and experience with hundreds of patients shows that if you continue to practice exposure and response prevention, your fears and compulsions will almost always decrease. But people's compulsions change at different rates. One person's fears may diminish in the first hour of practice, while a second person may feel better only after weeks of hard practice. There is nothing you can do about these differences, except to accept them as we accept individual differences in hair color and height. All that really matters is that with practice your fears will eventually subside. Habituation works in many areas of life apart from OCD. For example, most of us were afraid of the dark as children. We may have felt afraid, had urges to scream or cry, and suffered with thoughts of the bogeyman and other monsters hiding under our bed. As a result, we may have begged our parents to turn the lights on or to let us crawl into bed with them.

Over the months, if we—and our parents—persisted, and we continued to sleep in the dark, our fears and thoughts of bogeymen lessened. Thus, just by changing our *behavior* (staying in the dark room), we also indirectly changed our *thoughts* (monsters) and *feelings* (fear). Read the last sentence again; this is exactly what happens in all successful treatment for OCD.[1]

Exposure therapy, which is a first-line treatment for OCD, can easily be adapted to treat the sort of bad thoughts that are the subject of this book. The actual form of exposure therapy will always differ depending on the particular symptom to be treated, as well as the situations that trigger it. So for example, for a patient with OCD who has obsessive thoughts and performs no rituals, the target behaviors are the thoughts themselves. Often I can determine that the patient's bad thoughts are dependably triggered by specific situations, such as taking public transportation, going to a beach, or shopping in a particular store. For patients such as these, instructing them to actually enter these feared situations in real life (in technical terms this is "in vivo exposure") is usually effective. Many times, however, we must also supplement this in vivo exposure by having the person imagine facing the feared situations (i.e., imaginal exposure), often assisted by the use of a tape-recorded description of the feared situation. Both of these methods are described below, through actual case examples of people whose bad thoughts have been greatly reduced as a result.

In Vivo Exposure for Sexual Obsessions

Dr. Joseph Ciarrocchi, an expert in the treatment of religious obsessions at Loyola College in Maryland, recently described in elegant detail his successful exposure treatment of a patient with a strict religious upbringing who was suffering from sexual obsessions: .

A thirty-seven-year-old homosexual Baptist man who lived a celibate life was plagued by constant worries around intrusive sexual thoughts. Although he was physically attracted only to adult men, he had severe obsessions of pedophilia. Whenever he saw a handsome young man, he began to worry that he might not be older than eighteen years of age. He was so concerned about having sexual thoughts toward underage boys that he avoided looking at *any* man who was not obviously older than approximately thirty years of age. This obsession was most bothersome during church services, because the notion of having sexual thoughts about minors in church was horrific. As a result, he gazed with a fixed stare at the minister, lest his eyes wander and he be guilty of the sin of pedophilia.

Stage 1 of his exposure program involved obtaining a large department-store catalog. Therapist and patient then went through the fashions for adult men, selecting approximately ten pictures of men modeling business wear, casual wear, and beach attire. The patient then rank-ordered the pictures according to the degree of distress each picture generated, from least to most anxiety-provoking, with no large gaps in anxiety between any two pictures. Exposure then began in the therapist's office with the patient staring at the least anxiety-provoking picture until anxiety was sufficiently reduced. This process continued until desensitization was achieved for all the pictures.[2]

Stage 2 used the same catalog, but this time the pictures were selected from the adolescent fashion section. Again, the patient chose a range of pictures from dress clothes to beach wear, and exposure then proceeded in the same manner as described earlier. During both stages, the patient continued exposure trials at home, although it took several weeks of in vivo sessions before he had sufficient self-confidence to try it on his own.

Stage 3 involved in vivo exposure in natural environments. Now instead of avoiding looking at young men, the patient was instructed to actively seek them out and to look at them in a natural way.

Stage 4 involved performing the same in vivo exposure with adolescent men, and Stage 5 involved purposely looking at young men and teenage boys during church services. (Television programs often provide useful exposure trials, because scenes that scrupulous people avoid are readily available.)[3]

This is a classic example of the treatment of sexual bad thoughts by exposure therapy. Special considerations for dealing with bad thoughts that are entangled with religious beliefs (as in this patient) are covered in detail in the chapter on blasphemous bad thoughts.

In Vivo Exposure for Violent Obsessions

The treatment of violent thoughts by exposure therapy is similar to the treatment by Dr. Chiarrocchi in the case of sexual obsessions. In the case I describe below, I began by identifying situations that this man avoided because they triggered his violent thoughts. Then I helped him to confront them, until he habituated to them.

By the time Rick came to see me he was distraught. An anxious-appearing man in his midtwenties, he came to our clinic for help with thoughts about harming his parents and his girlfriend. At our first meeting, he told me that the harder he tried to resist these thoughts, the more upsetting and more persistent they seemed to become. He told me that he went out of his way to avoid any situation that would trigger his bad thoughts. When he was around his parents or his girlfriend, he was certain to clear the table of any pens, pencils, or other sharp objects that he feared he might attack her with. (When I later met his parents and his girlfriend, all confirmed that Rick was a gentle man who had never hurt a fly in his life, and whom all of them trusted completely, despite knowing all about his bad thoughts.)

Rick's problem had begun a year previously when, while out with friends and intoxicated, the thought passed through his mind, "How can be I sure that I don't really want to attack my friends?" This thought terrorized him, and although he told no one about it, it stuck with him and festered in his mind. Soon the thought spread to his parents, whom he lived with, with worries that he might stab them with scissors or a knife, and then to his girlfriend.

Rick had begun avoiding being around other people and was

no longer able to work. He told me that he had lost hope that he could ever again live a normal life, as he had just a year before. When I told him that with the proper treatment he had an excellent chance of recovery, he admitted that he couldn't believe me, but even though it sounded frightening, he would do his best to give it a try.

I began by explaining to Rick that the very act of avoiding his bad thoughts, along with situations that triggered them, was helping to keep them going. What we needed to do first was to discover all the situations he could think of that triggered his bad thoughts. Next, I would help him systematically expose himself to these situations. I told him that two decades of research had proven the best way to conquer our fears—even fears of our own thoughts and urges—is to expose ourselves to them. I explained that this results in habituation—that is, we get used to the situations so they no longer produce the high level of discomfort they once did, and the bad thoughts go down as well.

So before our next meeting Rick listed all the situations he could think of that triggered his bad thoughts. When he showed me his list, it included sitting close to his father or mother, being around them when sharp objects such as pencils or scissors were nearby, and sitting near his girlfriend, especially when sharp objects were around.

Now that we had identified situations that triggered his bad thoughts, I asked him to put himself in these situations as much as possible, and to remain in them even when he felt uncomfortable. When Rick returned, he told me that he had started off by sitting near his parents, which he had been avoiding. He told me that after he did this for a few nights, he began introducing sharp objects such as pens, pencils, knives, and scissors on a table within arm's reach of him while he sat and talked with his parents for at least an hour. He told me that each of these situations had produced extreme anxiety at first, but that this had gradually gone down as he continued practicing his exposure homework each day.

Next I asked Rick to stop avoiding his girlfriend, as he had been. At first, he simply sat closer and closer to her. Next, he gradually introduced sharp objects nearby. His girlfriend understood how exposure therapy was supposed to work and served as a cotherapist during the home exposure practices. She reminded Rick that the bad thoughts would pass through his mind from time to time, but that they were *just thoughts*, were probably due to his being overconscientious, and were not in themselves at all dangerous.

After three weeks of this practice, Rick told me he was feeling better and was able to be around people he had been avoiding. However, the bad thoughts were still occurring many times a day, and he asked me if there was anything he could do to make more progress.

I told Rick that to accelerate his progress he would have to expose himself to the very bad thoughts he was most afraid of. When he asked what I meant, I asked him to write down details of the very worst thoughts that tormented him. I told him these might be thoughts about "snapping" and stabbing his girlfriend with a knife; it might involve her parents coming upon the scene and accusing him of being insane; possibly he imagined the police would come and handcuff him and lead him to jail; he might see his face on the front page of the newspaper and a story describing him as the "insane sadistic killer"; possibly he feared being disowned by his family and dying alone and forgotten in a jail cell.

Like most of my patients, Rick's first reaction was to ask me if he really had to do this. I told him that this kind of exposure by audiotape has been found to be one of the most effective ways of dealing with bad thoughts like his. Rick gamely agreed to give it a try.

When he returned, he had done his homework and brought me a two-page script describing the worst scenario he could imagine. I reviewed his scenario with him to delete any reassurances he might have written in the script (including phrases like "but this will never really happen" or "God forgive me for doing this"). I crossed out all of these reassurances because they would undo the effects of the exposure tape.[4] When the script was complete, I had Rick record the horrible scenario on a cassette tape and instructed him to listen to it on a portable tape player for at least one hour a day, in addition to any other time the bad thoughts came. When he felt the thoughts coming, he was to sit down, put his headphones on, and listen to the exposure tape until the thoughts began to subside.

After two weeks of listening to this, and similar scenarios, Rick reported that his obsessions were occurring rarely, and he was easily able to tolerate them when they came. He was back at work and interacting normally with his parents and his girlfriend.

Rick's case illustrates that we often augment in vivo exposure therapy by other, less direct, exposure methods, when necessary. The following section describes the rationale for this approach, followed by additional examples of its use.

Using Audiotapes and Videotapes to Intensify Exposure Therapy

The catastrophes that are part of your bad thoughts will almost certainly never happen. Obviously you cannot do in vivo exposures for accidentally stabbing a baby or running over a pedestrian with your car! Even trying to imagine these catastrophes happening will often not be a useful exposure, since few of us have a vivid enough imagination, and even if we do, the temptation to distract our attention from such images may feel irresistible. Instead, many of my patients have successfully used videotapes to help rid them of generic bad thoughts, and audiotapes to help control idiosyncratic ones.

If you have violent or sexual bad thoughts, you probably go out of your way to avoid seeing television shows or movies with strong violent or sexual content. As you now know, avoiding triggers such as these only adds strength to your bad thoughts. For many of my patients, simply watching over and over videotapes with the particular content that triggers their bad thoughts will lead to habituation. For example, if you worry that you may inadvertently kill others, you could rent a videotape about a murderer that triggers your obsessions (such as Jeffrey Dahmer or Charles Manson); you would then sit and watch the videotape repeatedly until you find that your discomfort begins to go down (needless to say, you must also resist distracting yourself while watching the videotape).

Or, if you have bad thoughts about satanic possession, you could rent a video that triggers your obsessions about occult or supernatural events (such as *The Exorcist* or *Rosemary's Baby*), then watch it repeatedly from beginning to end until your distress begins to go down. I always know that exposure therapy is working when my patient tells me, "I can't stand watching that video one more time—it's just too boring!" I just smile, congratulate them, and remind them that boredom is the opposite of fear and means they are fully habituated.

On the other hand, the situations that trigger your bad thoughts may be personal and idiosyncratic. Anna worried that she would kill her infant son by touching him with hands contaminated by bacteria from uncooked meat or eggs. This had all but paralyzed her so that when she came for treatment, she refused to feed him or to change his diaper. Although in vivo exposure had enabled her to hold her son to feed and change him, her bad thoughts about killing him continued. For Anna, only a tailor-made audiotape would provide adequate exposure for her specific fears.

I convinced Anna that to complete her treatment she would have to expose herself to the *very catastrophe* she was most afraid of. She began by writing out for me, in excruciating detail, precisely the worst thing that she feared would happen to her infant. At our next session I reviewed what she'd written on two sheets of yellow legal paper, which I've paraphrased and shortened here to give you the flavor of an effective exposure script:

> I didn't wash my hands properly after cooking chicken. I feed my son, and later that day I notice he is not breathing right, as if his throat is closing up. I also take his temperature and he is getting a fever. I drive him to the emergency room and tell the doctor there what happened. He tells me that I probably gave my baby a bacterial infection and that he will probably not survive. I sit next to my baby's crib in the hospital and listen to him wheezing and having trouble breathing. He looks up at me with pleading eyes, and I know he's asking me to protect him and I know there's nothing I can do to help him. I cry continuously and feel more and

more helpless and guilty. Over the next several hours I see my son dying from this poison in his body that I gave him. Finally he dies a horrible death. My husband arrives at the hospital, and when he finds out what has happened, he yells at me hysterically and blames me for being an irresponsible mother who killed her own son. My mother and father tell me they want nothing more to do with me after I was so irresponsible in taking care of their grandson. My husband leaves me. I become homeless, live in a shelter, and become an alcoholic. After several years I realize there is nothing more to live for and I commit suicide.

When I read the first draft of Anna's script, I noticed that she had included several reassurances, which I pointed out to her and then crossed out (such phrases as "but I tell myself this really isn't happening" or "God forbid this would ever happen to him"). I told Anna that it would be uncomfortable for her to listen to this script at first; however, I assured her that as she listened to it over and over, it would eventually lose its ability to upset her. Then for the first time she could enjoy taking care of her son, which was Anna's original treatment goal. Anna then read her script into a tape recorder, repeating it three or four times until she had filled a thirty-minute side of a sixty-minute audiotape. She then slipped her tape into her portable tape player and listened to it for at least one hour every day. Happily, within a week, Anna told me that listening to the tape no longer produced strong discomfort, and soon the bad thoughts that had accompanied feeding and changing her son were almost gone. Now, a year later, she tells me that she and her son are doing well, and she is enjoying taking care of him and watching him grow up.[5]

Here is another example of using audiotapes to assist with exposure for fears of harming others:

Frieda had her first child late in life and came to see me because she was having difficulty feeling safe around her three-month-old child. Hers were the common fears of not wanting to change him when scissors or knives were around. But lately she had become even more distressed and no longer felt safe taking him outside for a walk because she suffered from images of pushing his carriage in front of an oncoming automobile, or throwing him from a bridge that she had formerly enjoyed crossing with him. Needless to say, Frieda was horrified by these thoughts, being, like most of my patients, overconscientious. She told me that since childhood she had always worried about doing the right thing, and now she worried about being the perfect mother and protecting her son, especially after waiting so long for his arrival. She had tried a variety of antianxiety and antidepressant medications over the past year, but none had reduced her bad thoughts, so her psychiatrist had referred her to me.

As she described her bad thoughts—and this was the first time she had ever told another person about them in detail—I listened intently, then assured her that I had no concern that she would ever act on her thoughts. She had no history of acting violently in the past, she seemed to have no trouble controlling her anger, and she was clearly not psychotic. These were purely obsessions, and she was far from being alone in suffering from them.

I then told Frieda that although I, too, wished we had an easier, more comfortable way of getting rid of her thoughts, the surest bet was for her to go through exposure therapy. I would help her to expose herself to the very bad thoughts and images that she been avoiding; she would not permit herself to turn off the thoughts and images to temporarily make herself feel better, since this would short-circuit the natural process of habituation.

I wasn't surprised to find that Frieda was exceptionally nervous the day I asked her to write out a detailed script about the worst consequence if her bad thoughts were to come true. I asked her to leave no stone unturned in making the script as vivid, as violent, and as detailed as a Stephen King horror story. The next week, she brought me three pages in her handwriting, carefully folded in an envelope with no identifying marks on the outside, and carefully hidden in her purse to ensure she wouldn't accidentally drop it.

Do not worry if, like Frieda, you feel guilty or ashamed about putting your bad thoughts on paper or audiotape. Most of my patients find this difficult, too. Some have told me they have burned the "evidence" at the conclusion of our treatment to ensure that it never "falls into the wrong hands"!

As I read her script, I saw that Frieda had done as I asked her and had produced a detailed script with no reassurances to decrease her distress. She told me that she had broken down into tears several times while committing these horrible thoughts to paper (the very writing down of these thoughts and images for the first time is often a powerful exposure for my patients).

She had written about taking her baby for a walk over the bridge; getting an urge to throw him over the side; giving in to the urge and flinging his light body down into the water; watching him fall through the air as if in slow motion, screaming and flailing his little arms; seeing her baby sink under the cold, dark water; bystanders screaming "Get her!" while she laughs insanely at the thought of her son drowning down below; being swarmed by a mob, grabbing and beating her; being brought to the police station; her picture flashed on the television news; facing her husband and his wrath; feeling shame and disgust at having committed this heinous crime; being beaten and raped by the other prisoners for being a child-killer; being disowned and forgotten by her family; having failed as a mother; becoming the monster she had always feared becoming; contracting AIDS in prison and dying, alone.

With my help, Frieda recorded this script onto an audiotape, which I asked her to listen to for one hour twice a day, and whenever else the bad thoughts popped up. The first time she listened to the tape in my office, she broke into tears but forced herself to listen to it, rating herself as a ten out of ten on a scale of anxiety. I reassured her that if she continued to listen to the tape, her distress would start to decrease, and the bad thoughts would gradually lose their terror for her.

At first, Frieda had to force herself to use the tape, but she kept her promise to me and listened to it on a regular schedule. By the end of the first week she noticed the start of a drop in her distress. This decrease continued through the second week, and by the time she returned to see me after the third week, Frieda reported that, to her surprise, the tape was beginning to bore her! Later I helped Frieda make two additional tapes for exposure to other bad thoughts she had about pushing her son into traffic and of stabbing him. As she continued to listen to these tapes and began to habituate, I encouraged her to resume taking her son for walks. With this combined audiotape and in vivo exposure treatment, by the end of six weeks Frieda didn't avoid any situations with her son, and she enjoyed being with him, without the horrid thoughts. Occasionally, a bad thought would still pass through her mind, but since she now realized that this was "just a thought" and of no importance, she simply let it pass through her mind without fighting it. I'm pleased that she continues to be much improved more than two years later.

Should you expect to be completely cured by exposure therapy? No. Few patients find that their thoughts are completely eliminated. But the majority find that their bad thoughts are decreased significantly by exposure therapy, and that they do not interfere with their lives nearly as much after treatment. If you decide to try exposure therapy, I have listed in tables 9 and 10 some sample in vivo exposure tasks and topics for audiotapes that my colleagues and I have used with our patients to help you get started in planning your own exposure practices. Some of these examples may seem shocking or morally wrong to you. You will learn in chapter 7 what to do if an exposure task that might help you seems morally wrong to you.

TABLE 9
ACTUAL TASKS USED IN IN VIVO EXPOSURE THERAPY FOR BAD THOUGHTS[6]

Thoughts about harming children	• offer to baby-sit alone for a child
	• offer to bathe or diaper a child
	• obtain information on abortion services
	• do not check trash or toilet (when afraid child was placed there)
	• do reading on history of abortion (e.g., Roe vs. Wade case)
	• walk by an abortion clinic
	• read newspaper article on parent who physically abused her child
	• locate phone number for abortion services

Religious obsessions (about devil worship)	• write the words "Satan" and "Devil" • role-play membership in satanic cult • read about devil-worship rites • search Internet for information on satanic cults
Obsessions about becoming homosexual	• walk around gay neighborhood • read autobiography of gay person • attend gay rights rally • look at nude or semi-nude pictures of same sex in catalogs or magazines such as *Playboy* • use open dressing room in gym or clothing store • look at nude portraits in museums and art books
Obsessions about incest	• make flattering comment to male relative ("You look good in that sweater") • give male relative a hug or kiss • have underwear touch objects father had touched
Sexual obsessions	• sit facing other people • eat a "dirty" food (i.e., penis-shaped: banana, zucchini, cucumber) • write "sexual" words (e.g., *come, get into, swallowing*) • go to a location where there are children (mall arcade, food court) to confront sexual fears about children • listen to audiotape with intrusive sexual and violent obsessions (can increase difficulty by listening at a church or around children)

TABLE 10
ACTUAL TEXT OF EXPOSURE AUDIOTAPES FOR BAD THOUGHTS

Bad thoughts about exposing himself and having sex with bypassers:

I might have an erection. I might get AIDS. I might get AIDS. I'm not sure if I am wearing pants or not. I might take off my pants. I'm not sure if I am wearing pants or not. I might get AIDS. I'm probably going to get AIDS. I'm going to rape someone. I'm going to start masturbating. I'm going to start getting undressed. I was going to the bathroom. I'm going to get interrupted. I might have AIDS. I'm going to get AIDS. I'm going to get AIDS. I'm not sure if I got interrupted or not while I was getting dressed, or when I was going to the bathroom, or when I was masturbating. I could get AIDS. I could get AIDS. I could get AIDS.

Bad thoughts about killing a child:

I am walking over the bridge and I get an urge to throw my child into the water below. I take her out of her carriage, and with her looking at me trustingly, I throw her down over the railing, watching her sink into the cold water below. Many witnesses see me do this and scream to stop the madwoman, but they are helpless to save my daughter.

Bad thoughts about losing control and stabbing a loved one:

I am sitting across from my girlfriend and I see a knife on the table. I pick it up and snap, stabbing her with it over and over. My worst fears have come true as I continue stabbing her to death.

Bad thoughts about blasphemy:

I am in church, shouting obscenities to God and Jesus. I rip the crucifix off the wall and smash it to pieces while the congregation looks on at me in amazement.

Bad thoughts about sex with animals:

I see the dog's genitals and to my horror get sexually excited. I snap and grab the dog and begin having anal intercourse with him. My mother comes into my room and is horrified at what she sees, but I just continue on, the fear I've had for so many years finally coming true.

Bad thoughts about incest:
    I am having sex with my sister. I have lost control of my senses as I feared I would and am now engaging in the worst thing I can imagine. (Continues describing in great detail.)

Bad thoughts about harming and molesting family members:
    I want to suffocate my son with a pillow while he's sleeping. I want to shoot him in the back of his head on his bald spot with a gun. I want to knife my mother. I want to stab my father. I want to have sex with my father. I want to kiss my sister in the crotch and have oral sex with her. I want to kill my husband. I'm going to have sex with a child. I will have sensations and masturbate around children. I think I harmed a child. I should be killed. I'm a bad mother. I deserve no mercy.

Unfortunately, some people do not respond to exposure therapy, even when they cooperate fully with it, and others are not willing to attempt it. For them, other treatments such as cognitive therapy and medication treatments may be helpful.

Before you try exposure therapy on your own, refer back to page 43 in chapter three and review the warning signs for when bad thoughts may be dangerous, to make sure it's safe for you to proceed. If you are not sure whether your bad thoughts are true or not, or if you have tried exposure therapy for at least ten hours and have not noticed any decrease in your anxiety, you should next try the cognitive therapy techniques described in the next chapter. If after using these techniques you still have not noticed any decrease in your symptoms, then it is time to consult a mental health professional. It might be that you need to be prescribed one of the medications described in chapter 8.

Fortunately, most people who suffer from bad thoughts are able to benefit from exposure therapy. Several studies have found that exposure therapy can be just as effective when it is self-administered as when a therapist is involved. However, this requires that you expose yourself to the correct triggers, and that you continue the exposure long enough—and without any rituals or distractions—for habituation to happen. You may want to find a trusted friend or family member to help you with this approach if you find that you cannot do it on your own. In fact, even if you can do the exposure on your own, because of the shame and guilt associated with these bad thoughts, I suggest you find someone to talk to about them. Just talking about them can be an effective exposure and can greatly decrease your guilt. If a support group exists in your area for problems like these, this can be an excellent treatment option. Of course, if your problem is severe, you should consult a qualified mental health professional.

6

Questioning Your Bad Thoughts: Cognitive Therapy

Be not swept off your feet by the vividness of the impression,
but say, "Impression, wait for me a little. Let me see what you
are and what you represent."

—Epictetus (c. 55–135)

While exposure therapy remains the treatment of choice for bad
thoughts, over the past decade an additional treatment has become available. Called cognitive therapy, it is for those unable or
unwilling to undergo exposure therapy. The idea has always been
attractive: *Since obsessions are composed of thoughts that are, on
the face of them, irrational, why can't a sufferer learn how to directly change these thoughts?* But, as usual, the practice proved
much more difficult than the theory would have predicted.

Early attempts to modify cognitive therapy, a treatment first
proven effective for depression, for the treatment of OCD were
generally unsuccessful. Initially, researchers attempted to directly
apply the methods developed by Dr. Aaron Beck at the University of Pennsylvania to teach patients how to identify and to
modify irrational thoughts that led to depression.[1] After several
studies with only mixed results, Drs. Patricia van Oppen and Paul
Emmelkamp, working in the Netherlands, wondered whether cognitive therapy might prove more effective for OCD if it was
tailored specifically to the irrational thoughts that are characteristic of this disorder—rather than using the standard depression-
treatment program as had been done before.

The researchers surveyed many OCD patients and found a number of common kinds of irrational thoughts, including mistakes such as overestimating the chances of danger and feeling overly responsible for the results of their actions. Based on their studies, they developed a cognitive therapy treatment program tailored specifically for OCD and began studies comparing this new method to our gold standard treatment of exposure therapy, and also to a placebo treatment. Shockingly, to those of us who view exposure therapy as the bedrock of treatment for OCD, they found that cognitive therapy—that is, teaching patients how to *directly* change their thoughts—was as effective as exposure treatment, and both were far more effective than the placebo.

Because cognitive therapy seemed to hold promise as a treatment that might be helpful for those of our patients who were unwilling or unable to undergo exposure therapy, several of my colleagues at Massachusetts General Hospital, headed by Dr. Sabine Wilhelm, translated the cognitive therapy treatment manual from the original Dutch into English and began studying this treatment for our OCD patients in Boston. Encouragingly, this treatment appears to be especially helpful for patients suffering from the type of bad thoughts that are the subject of this book. It now seems likely that by teaching patients about their own thought processes, and how to test them for rationality, many patients are able to get their bad thoughts under control.

Before giving you an example of how cognitive therapy is used to treat a particular bad thought (in this case, about incest), it is important to understand the theory underlying this treatment.

The Cognitive Theory of Obsessions[2]

Cognitive therapy for treating obsessions is based on the idea that intrusive thoughts are occurrences that everybody experiences. According to this theory, the person who suffers from OCD does not differ from one without OCD in the content of her thoughts (after all, everyone has violent or sexual thoughts from time to time), but simply in *the way she reacts to and interprets her thoughts.* While most people are able to ignore intrusive thoughts and recognize them as unimportant, the person with OCD pays too much attention to them and interprets them as very important. Cognitive therapists assume that the person with OCD pays too much attention to her thoughts because of beliefs that she learned earlier in life in church, school, or in her family. Also, if she underestimates her ability to cope with intrusive thoughts, she will probably try to suppress her intrusive thoughts—which we now know will actually only give her bad thoughts added strength! To make matters worse, she will probably begin to avoid situations that trigger her bad thoughts, making a bad situation even worse. As we've seen, although thought suppression is a common strategy to get rid of intrusive thoughts, the approach usually backfires, since many studies have found that when we try to suppress thoughts—especially emotionally charged ones—these thoughts will occur more, rather than less often.

Researchers from around the world have recently classified the most common cognitive errors in OCD into the categories listed in Table 11.

TABLE 11
Cognitive Errors Common Among Those with Obsessions

- attributing too much importance to having a particular thought
- thinking they need to be able to completely control their thoughts
- thinking a situation is more dangerous than it really is
- intolerance of uncertainty—wanting to have total certainty
- perfectionism—wanting to do things perfectly to avoid any criticism from others
- excessive responsibility—believing you have the ultimate responsibility and power to prevent bad things from happening

Modified from: Wilhelm, S. "Cognitive Therapy for Obsessive-Compulsive Disorder," *Journal of Cognitive Psychotherapy,* 14 (2000): 43.

In cognitive therapy treatment, the therapist assesses which of these areas a patient is having problems in, then addresses these areas with specific procedures (described later in this chapter).

Overimportance of Thoughts and the Need to Control Them

This cognitive error occurs when we conclude that simply because we have a particular thought, it must be meaningful. Similarly, we may conclude that simply because we are thinking about something, this means that it will actually happen. If we have this mistaken belief about the importance of thoughts, we may start to believe that we have to exercise complete control over all our thoughts (which unfortunately, as we have seen, is doomed to fail).

Overestimating Danger

People with OCD often overestimate both the likelihood and the dangerousness of things that may happen. They often view a situation as threatening until they are guaranteed that it is safe. Most people without OCD, on the other hand, assume that a situation is safe unless it is proven to be dangerous.

Intolerance of Uncertainty

Perhaps because people with OCD tend to overestimate the likelihood of danger, they often have trouble making decisions in uncertain or ambiguous situations, then subsequently question whether their decision was correct. Several researchers have found a connection between perfectionism, concern over mistakes, doubts about actions, and OCD symptoms.

Perfectionism

Several studies of OCD have found a connection between inability to tolerate uncertainty and perfectionism. For instance, OCD sufferers believe that their actions must be perfect if they are to avoid criticism from others.

Excessive Responsibility

If you believe that you have the primary power and responsibility to make sure bad things don't happen, then you probably commit this cognitive error. Since many, if not most, outcomes in life are beyond our control, excessive responsibility will often lead to guilt when bad things happen to us or our loved ones (even when in reality we had no control to avert these things).

CASE EXAMPLE: COGNITIVE THERAPY FOR SEXUAL OBSESSIONS

To illustrate how the cognitive distortions listed above are addressed in cognitive therapy, I asked Dr. Wilhelm to discuss a patient who used cognitive therapy to control bad thoughts. She told me about a young man she had recently seen who had done well with brief cognitive therapy, and whose treatment illustrated its various elements. Charles had come to see Dr. Wilhelm for help with upsetting thoughts about incest with his mother, which had worsened over the past year to the point where he could hardly do anything because the thoughts bothered him so much. When he first came to the clinic, he tried to tense all his muscles to push the thoughts out of his mind, and he had not eaten for two days, because he didn't want to allow himself any pleasure, and because he thought that doing anything pleasurable—from buying new clothes to sexual activity—would bring on the bad thoughts and had to be avoided. Dr. Wilhelm had only two months to work with Charles because he was leaving on an extended trip to his home country. After only eight sessions of cognitive therapy, Charles noted a marked reduction in his bad thoughts about incest, which remained low even during a visit to his family, when he was able to be around his mother with little difficulty.

Dr. Wilhelm told me that the single most important element in Charles's rapid progress was simply his understanding the cognitive theory of obsessions. For example, she believes that no technique was as powerful for Charles as his learning about the studies showing that everybody has bad thoughts about violence and sex from time to time. Just understanding that *everybody* has weird thoughts, and that the only way that he was different was in how he was reacting to these thoughts, was a revelation to Charles. For years he had been thinking that he was having incestuous thoughts because he was either an evil person or a sexual monster. Now he learned this wasn't true! He had convinced himself that because he was thinking these incestuous thoughts, one day he would surely act on them. But he learned that this, too, was untrue!

These realizations began to free Charles from the self-imposed prison his life had become. Before treatment, his life had gotten more and more constricted in an attempt to avoid the sexual thoughts; when he came to treatment, he was trying to avoid *all* women. Dr. Wilhelm emphasized how relieved Charles was to learn that his problem was *not* to force himself never to have thoughts about sex (even from time to time passing thoughts of sex with family members), but rather not to beat himself up unmercifully for his thoughts. This was so helpful to Charles that Dr. Wilhelm and he reviewed this idea frequently throughout their eight sessions.

When he first came to see Dr. Wilhelm for treatment, Charles was not able to shop, only ate when his wife was around, and rarely socialized. If a bad thought came to him while he was doing something pleasurable, that activity would immediately be "ruined" for him. He went out of his way avoid any activities during which he had ever had a bad thought.

At his first session, Charles told Dr. Wilhelm that his bad thoughts occurred almost constantly all through the day. The thoughts were upsetting and interfered with his concentration both at work and at home. (He also disclosed fears about becoming contaminated and washing excessively. He was also disgusted with bodily wastes and with insects, and he avoided public rest rooms. Nevertheless, Charles told Dr. Wilhelm that these other problems were far overshadowed by his bad thoughts about incest.)

Charles had never before had any psychiatric treatment and didn't want to take medications. His marriage was intact, except that his wife was becoming frustrated with his OCD symptoms. Charles described his father as having "very high moral standards," and his mother as "a saint" and the person he loved and respected the most. As usual in his country, discussions about sexual topics were taboo in the home while he was growing up.

Being strongly influenced by his religious upbringing, Charles believed strongly that he should not have bizarre sexual thoughts and thus felt guilty and ashamed about the incestuous thoughts about his mother and sister. He told Dr. Wilhelm that *if only he could exercise enough willpower, he should be able to control his bad thoughts*, and he became anxious when his attempts to stop the intrusive thoughts failed.

Charles believed that having sexual thoughts like these indicated that he was a bad person, and that a catastrophe would happen if he was unable to control his thoughts. Finally, Charles believed that he could never have peace of mind so long as he had the bad thoughts. To make matters worse, Charles thought it was dangerous to permit his bad thoughts to come and go naturally, so he attempted to suppress them. As Dr. Wilhelm sat listening to Charles's story with the ears of a cognitive therapist, she recognized that his set of misconceptions and beliefs had left him vulnerable to interpreting his bad thoughts in a way that was destined to lead to anxiety and guilt. Below is a detailed description of how she used a variety of cognitive therapy techniques to correct these misconceptions and irrational beliefs.

Treatment

At first, Charles was embarrassed when he talked about his bad thoughts. To help him feel more comfortable, Dr. Wilhelm tried to be encouraging, warm, and nonjudgmental. She showed confidence that the cognitive treatment would be helpful and stressed how important it was for the two of them to collaborate in the treatment.

In the first treatment session Charles learned about the cognitive theory for OCD. Dr. Wilhelm gave him a new way of looking at his bad thoughts—specifically, that rather than being an unusual bizarre symptom, intrusive bad thoughts were actually common experiences that most people have (at this point Dr. Wilhelm told Charles about the studies of normal college students

in several countries confirming that bad thoughts are universal).
She then helped Charles to become more aware of the circumstances that influenced his negative interpretations of his bad
thoughts (such as his past experiences in his family, whether he
was feeling anxious or depressed, recent stressors in his life) and
taught him about the dangers of avoidance and thought suppression in unwittingly maintaining obnoxious obsessions.

In subsequent treatment sessions Charles acquired skills to
recognize maladaptive appraisals and reactions to intrusive thoughts
and learned to develop alternative interpretations of intrusions,
assisted by the Socratic questioning technique. Examples included "Is your appraisal of the intrusion helpful right now?
Is your appraisal realistic? What would you tell another OCD
patient about this?" Charles was also taught how to fill out a
thought record, which helped him to identify his irrational and
negative appraisals of bad thoughts and to learn to develop more
rational alternatives. He completed these thought records both
during treatment sessions and as homework assignments.

From the thought records he had been keeping, Charles and
Dr. Wilhelm determined which cognitive distortions were most
problematic for him. They then decided to first tackle Charles's
need to control his thoughts and his overestimating of their importance, since these were the areas in which Charles had the
most severe problems. Later, they addressed Charles's tendency
to overestimate the probability and severity of danger.

Throughout the eight sessions, Dr. Wilhelm taught Charles a
variety of cognitive techniques. Some addressed several cognitive
distortions, such as making a list of advantages and disadvantages
of believing in a certain interpretation. Other techniques were
relevant only for a specific distortion, such as the thought suppression test to show firsthand the paradoxical effects of trying to
control one's own thoughts. Between sessions, Charles carried
out experiments to test for himself the material discussed in the
sessions.

The final session focused on learning how to prevent a relapse
of symptoms in the future. Dr. Wilhelm explained that obsessions would probably flare up from time to time, but that Charles

would know how to cope with them. She advised him to keep working on his thoughts after the end of treatment and discussed techniques to handle setbacks and relapses.

Below is a detailed description of the specific cognitive techniques that Charles learned during his treatment sessions. If you have bad thoughts, you may find that trying these strategies will help you as well.

Thought Suppression Experiment

According to the cognitive theory, Charles's sexual thoughts had become a problem *because of the way he was reacting to them.* Because Charles believed that his intrusive bad thoughts were important and unacceptable, he was greatly bothered by them, and so he tried to suppress them. Sadly, he learned that it is nearly impossible to suppress our thoughts.

To teach firsthand how difficult it is to control our thoughts, Dr. Wilhelm asked Charles to *think about a giraffe continuously for one full minute* (have someone time you with a watch if you are trying this exercise). He was told to lift his finger *anytime the giraffe disappeared from his mind.* As Dr. Wilhelm expected, Charles found it difficult to concentrate on the giraffe for the whole minute, and he lifted his finger over and over. Next, Dr. Wilhelm reversed her instructions and told Charles *to not think about the giraffe for one full minute* and to lift his finger anytime a giraffe thought came into his mind. Once again Charles lifted his finger over and over. In fact, Charles's attempt to suppress giraffe thoughts actually resulted in more rather than fewer of these thoughts. They then discussed implications of the thought suppression experiment and Charles's efforts to suppress his intrusive sexual thoughts. Charles agreed that experience showed that thought suppression was not an effective approach, since it made thoughts occur more frequently.

Education About How Our Thoughts and Emotions Work (Psychoeducation)

Charles's beliefs about his obsessions were normalized by educating him about how sexual thoughts, fantasies, and arousal

really work. He learned, for example, that we all might find ourselves thinking about, or being aroused by, a wide range of things,
including some unrelated to sexual behavior. Dr. Wilhelm encouraged him to get sex education books from the library to
learn more about common sexual fantasies and the physiology of
arousal. At first he was too embarrassed to read about these topics, but he soon overcame this and read several books that reduced his catastrophic interpretations of his sexual fantasies.

The "Downward Arrow" Technique

Charles found the downward arrow technique particularly
beneficial for his recovery.[3] After he had identified a particular intrusive bad thought, Dr. Wilhelm kept pressing him about the
meaning or significance of that intrusive thought. "And if that
thought were true, what would it mean?" she kept asking, until
Charles's fundamental beliefs were disclosed. Table 12 lists
Charles's bad thoughts and the underlying beliefs that were identified by using the downward arrow technique.

TABLE 12
THE DOWNWARD ARROW TECHNIQUE

Images and thoughts about sex with mother

⇩

These thoughts are disgusting

⇩

I need to get rid of these thoughts

⇩

If I cannot control these thoughts, I might act on them

⇩

I am evil

Assessing Advantages and Disadvantages of Bad Thoughts

Dr. Wilhelm asked Charles to question his belief that he needed to suppress the kind of bad thoughts that were identified by the downward arrow technique.

Here, Charles listed the advantages and all the disadvantages he could think of that came to him from believing that he *should* control these thoughts. Next Dr. Wilhelm helped Charles to check the validity of each of the advantages he listed through a question-and-answer approach called the Socratic method. This technique convinced Charles that he would be far better off to stop trying so hard to control his bad thoughts (since this was a losing battle that was causing him more disadvantages than advantages), a change that led to a substantial drop in his obsessions.

Examining the Evidence by Performing Behavioral Experiments

Using the downward arrow technique revealed that one of Charles's most frightening beliefs was that he would eventually act on the incestuous thoughts if he was not able to control them. Dr. Wilhelm helped Charles challenge this assumption by demonstrating from everyday examples that thinking about something does not make it more likely to happen. Whether riding a train and thinking about sticking his tongue out, or sitting in the waiting room and thinking about throwing all the magazines in the garbage can—Charles agreed that thinking about these things did not really make them more likely to happen. Next Charles was asked to carry out behavioral experiments to test this theory. For example, Charles was to try thinking about dancing in the nude in the clinic's waiting room to see if this would lead him to actually do this (he didn't!).

He was asked to view these as experiments in which he was playing the role of a scientist collecting evidence that would either support or disprove his hypothesis. So, like a scientist, Charles began by noting his prediction (e.g., "If I think of something sexual, immoral, or embarrassing, I will not be able to resist doing it") and also rating the strength of his belief in this theory. After the experiment was completed, Charles and Dr. Wilhelm reviewed his initial prediction and compared it with the results of the experiment. Through this scientific process, Charles began to understand that his theories and predictions did not hold up to the objective evidence. Thinking about something did *not* inevitably make it happen. As a result he was gradually forced to change his beliefs to agree with the evidence he had gathered in his experiments.

Questioning Basic Beliefs

During the downward arrow procedure, the belief "I am evil" emerged. The therapist assisted Charles to become aware of this strongly held belief and then carefully introduced the idea that a more accurate belief might be "I am extremely worried about acting immorally and hurting my mother." Together, Charles and Dr. Wilhelm examined whether any evidence, apart from the intrusive thoughts, suggested that Charles was evil. Next they investigated whether any evidence suggested that Charles was not evil. This strategy helped Charles to see himself in a more realistic way, and he gradually concluded that the belief that he was evil was not accurate.

Cognitive Continuum Technique

Another effective technique to challenge the belief that Charles was evil was the cognitive continuum technique.[4] On a scale from 0 (most moral person ever) to 100 (most immoral/evil person ever), Charles rated how evil he was for thinking about sex with his mother. Then Dr. Wilhelm asked him to rate how bad/immoral a mass murderer is, or a rapist. After each new example Charles rerated his own badness for simply thinking about sex with his mother. Eventually Charles realized that having an intrusive thought about his mother was relatively harmless and not nearly as "evil" as he had appraised it initially.

Calculating the True Probability of Danger

As mentioned earlier, although less severe than his sexual obsessions, Charles had contamination and illness fears, and related cleaning rituals. The techniques and behavioral experiments described above were also used to treat contamination and illness fears. Dr. Wilhelm taught Charles to contrast his original esti-

mate of harm to the multiplied estimations of the entire sequence of events that would be necessary to result in the feared
outcome. First, Charles estimated the probability of negative
outcomes. In collaboration with the therapist, he then estab-
lished each of the individual steps that would have to take place
to result in the dangerous outcome. Next Charles was asked to
estimate the chance of each of these individual events occurring separately. With the help of a calculator, Charles then calculated the final cumulative probability by multiplying all of the
probabilities of each individual event. Finally, Charles and the
therapist compared this probability estimate to Charles's initial
estimate. Table 13 shows that Charles's original estimate of the
probability of developing AIDS by shaking his dentist's hand was
thirty percent. He and Dr. Wilhelm then discussed that the
following sequence of steps would have to occur for Charles to
develop AIDS.

TABLE 13
CALCULATING THE TRUE PROBABILITY OF DANGER

Event	Chance of this event occuring	Cumulative chance of all events[5]
(1) The dentist must have HIV-positive blood on his hands	1/1,000	1/1,000
(2) I came in touch with the virus while shaking his hand	1/10	1/10,000
(3) My skin was broken at the point of contact	1/10	1/100,000
(4) The virus generates HIV	1/10	1/1,000,000
(5) HIV develops into AIDS	1/10	1/10,000,000

After completing this process, Charles was surprised to find
how low the real chance of danger—.00001 percent as calculated
from his own estimates—compared to his original estimate of
thirty percent!

Outcome of Treatment

Charles's pretreatment score on the YBOCS was thirty-five, indicating that his OCD was very severe. However, immediately after treatment his YBOCS score had dropped to eighteen, thus showing considerable improvement. With a symptom reduction of nearly fifty percent he was considered a treatment responder. Overall, Charles rated himself as "much improved" at the end of treatment.

Charles returned two months after the end of treatment and was clearly continuing to improve. His YBOCS score had dropped to eight, indicating he had only mild OCD symptoms. Overall, Charles rated himself as "very much improved."

Although we are encouraged by our early studies with cognitive therapy for bad thoughts, exposure therapy remains the first-line nondrug treatment for this problem. On the other hand, if someone suffering from bad thoughts is unwilling or unable to do the necessary exposure tasks, then cognitive therapy gives us another useful approach to try. As an example, Dr. Wilhelm told me that although Charles's sexual obsessions may have responded just as well to exposure to being around his mother—perhaps supplemented with an audiotape containing an incestuous scenario, as described in chapter 5—she doubts that he would have been willing to fully comply with this approach.

In a recent survey in our clinic, Dr. Wilhelm discovered that many of her patients find the cognitive therapy approach more acceptable as a first step in treatment. Later, as they understand more about their thoughts and beliefs, many are willing to do exposure tasks. Happily, though, some patients' bad thoughts have responded well to the cognitive therapy approach alone, such as one of Dr. Wilhelm's patients suffering from intrusive thoughts that she might be gay—for this woman, simply understanding the cognitive theory of why she had these thoughts was enough for her to rapidly get relief from them.

You may have already noticed that, in reality, it is usually impossible to do cognitive therapy without including some elements of exposure. In Charles's case, for example, discussing his incestuous thoughts with Dr. Wilhelm was a form of exposure, and no doubt resulted in habituation of his anxiety and shame about them. This is one reason why I suggest that even if you try to control your bad thoughts alone, you should try to find someone you trust enough to tell about your thoughts—this can be a health professional, a friend, a family member, or a religious adviser.

In summary, our early studies of cognitive therapy for bad thoughts suggest this will be a useful treatment. On the other hand, we have not yet studied the effectiveness of this approach when it is self-administered. So if you think you might benefit from this treatment, but you find that you are not able to use the methods outlined in this chapter to help yourself, you should seek out a qualified mental health professional with experience in this kind of treatment to help you.

7

Blasphemous Bad Thoughts

No disease of the imagination . . . is so difficult to cure, as
that which is complicated with the dread of guilt: fancy and
conscience then act interchangeably upon us . . . the
superstitious are often melancholy, and the melancholic
almost always superstitious.

—Samuel Johnson (1709–1784)

Martin Luther was tormented by urges to curse God and Jesus.
While praying he was obsessed with images of "the Devil's behind."[1] St. Ignatius could not step on two pieces of straw if
they formed a cross, lest he show disrespect to Christ crucified.[2]
Robert Burton, in his classic book *The Anatomy of Melancholy*, wrote in 1621 of an unfortunate fellow who, "if he was in a
silent auditorium as at a sermon, he was afraid he shall speak
aloud at unawares, something indecent, unfit to be said." And
John Moore, the bishop of Norwich, preached before Queen Mary
II in 1691 on "religious melancholy," describing good moral wor-
shipers who are tormented by "naughty and sometimes blasphemous thoughts"—despite all their efforts to stifle and suppress
them."[3]

When bad thoughts take on religious implications, suffering is
often greater, and treatment complicated. That is why I have held
off discussing this complicated "special case" of bad thoughts
until having introduced the standard treatments.

No one has more experience treating religious bad thoughts
than Dr. William E. Minichiello, my longtime friend and mentor
at Massachusetts General Hospital. With a background as a

Catholic priest, as well as decades of experience in treating people with obsessions, Dr. Minichiello has a unique perspective on these issues. Consequently I frequently refer my patients with religious concerns about bad thoughts to him for one or more sessions. The most common problem he sees in patients troubled by blasphemous thoughts is what he calls "a totally untheological view of God."

Not long ago I referred Janie—the young woman suffering from both bad thoughts and PTSD flashbacks—to speak with Dr. Minichiello about her belief that she was doomed to spend eternity in hell. Janie had been raised Catholic, had attended Mass every Sunday morning with her family, and had been taught that evil thoughts were just as sinful as evil acts. Because of her evil thoughts she had believed for as long as she could remember that she was headed to hell after she died. To help Janie feel more comfortable in her first meeting with Dr. Minichiello, I sat in to introduce them and then listened to the conversation. Dr. Minichiello's warmth, kindness, and wisdom gradually put Janie at ease, and she was soon asking him questions she had yearned to ask for years.

To correct what he called Janie's untheological view of God, Dr. Minichiello started by trying to convince her that God is not a monster. He is not like a human who gets angry and retaliates. Instead, Dr. Minichiello emphasized to Janie over and over that the Scriptures describe a God of love. Since Janie was a Christian, he asked her, "How do we know God? We know God through Jesus—and what was Jesus' description of the father? A God of love." He gave her examples such as the parable of the prodigal son: Despite all the wrong things the prodigal son had done, his father forgave him totally and ordered a great celebration for the son whom he had believed was lost forever. Dr. Minichiello's message to Janie was that He is a God of love—love with no strings attached—unconditional love. Dr. Minichiello patiently answered each of Janie's questions, always reassuring that she is not going to lose God's love unless she makes a *deliberate* choice to do something she knows to be evil, such as commit murder, and then remains unrepentant. He contrasted this with Janie's bad thoughts, which aren't sinful by these criteria, but rather are the product of a brain disorder, OCD. As she told him about each of her thoughts, he reassured her that there was nothing sinful about having them—even the most violent or perverse ones. Nothing, he told her, was going to sever her relationship with God. Most importantly, Dr. Minichiello reassured Janie that her thoughts have nothing to do with her as a person—they are simply the result of the disorder that she suffers from. He pointed out that, unlike her, people who are truly violent *are not bothered* by these kind of bad thoughts. We could view what Dr. Minichiello did with Janie as a special case of the cognitive therapy described earlier—one carried out by spiritual advisers for most of human history.

I met with Janie after her meeting with Dr. Minichiello, and she told me she felt a little less certain that she was destined for hell, and less afraid. In the weeks that followed, she began discussing her fears further with a priest that Dr. Minichiello recommended, and she now feels confident enough to begin confronting her bad thoughts directly with exposure therapy without considering them sins. Although she has a long way to go, Janie tells me she now feels hope for the first time in a long while.

Later, when I discussed Janie's case with Dr. Minichiello, he reminded me that we must always remember that people like Janie are usually *sensitive* people, with a *sensitive* sense of God. As I listened, I thought back to my group members and their childhoods as highly *sensitive* and conscientious children (which I described in chapter 4). The pieces seemed to fit—perhaps this is why they are so unforgiving of themselves as adults.

Religious obsessions have a unique quality that Dr. Minichiello cautions must always be kept in mind. He gives as an example a Christian patient suffering from true blasphemous obsessions or urges. The patient believed these thoughts were inspired by Satan—thinking "I hate God," having sexual thoughts or images about religious figures, thoughts of desecrating the bread and wine of the Eucharist, or urges to tear down and smash the crucifix. Usually, when I do exposure therapy, I tell the patient that by exposing himself to the feared situation he will discover that nothing bad will happen. But, in Dr. Minichiello's example, the patient feared that the punishment might be long delayed, perhaps until after his death. Because we are talking about the after-life, which cannot be directly tested, the patient must have faith in what Dr. Minichiello and other religious advisers say, before the patient is willing to do exposure therapy.

On the other hand, Dr. Minichiello warns that if Janie did not have this faith, but continued to believe that her thoughts and exposure exercises were demonic or sinful, then he would *never encourage her to do exposure therapy to such things*. He has seen too many cases where forcing patients to do this has made them worse, as with his example of the man who was *truly afraid* of per-forming satanic acts. Dr. Minichiello cautions therapists to first make certain that the patient doesn't *truly believe* the exposure tasks are sinful, before encouraging him to do any exposure—our responsibility, after Hippocrates, must always be to first do no harm. The key question Dr. Minichiello always keeps in mind is "Do you truly believe that God is going to punish you for having your thoughts?"

Another expert in religious obsessions, Dr. Joseph Ciarrocchi at Loyola College in Maryland, recently echoed Dr. Minichiello's observations in our textbook on OCD:

> The more intractable symptoms in OCD often fall under the rubric of overvalued ideas. Overvalued ideas occupy a midway point between reality and delusion—ideas firmly held but with a tinge of uncertainty as to their truth. Reli-gious obsessions and compulsions, because they involve the ethical dimension for people, frequently fall into this cate-gory of overvalued ideas.[4]

In other words, bad thoughts involving religion can be espe-cially difficult to treat if the sufferer *truly* fears God's punishment of eternal damnation. If so, the shame of having bad thoughts is magnified because of their perceived sinfulness, and they are rarely shared with another human being. In cases such as these, medication treatments are rarely effective unless the shame and guilt are relieved through counseling.

In Dr. Ciarrocchi's experience, many patients, due to their

religious beliefs, are unwilling to engage in the exposure therapy they need to get better. For example, some of his patients with religious obsessions see their thoughts and feelings (anger, jealousy, or sexual arousal) as *equivalent to performing the act they think about*. They then worry that an exposure exercise such as looking at pictures of partially clothed people in a department store catalog constitutes "adultery of the heart" and thus are unwilling to do it. To avoid this problem, Dr. Ciarrocchi often lists the exposure tasks he has and then has his patient take this list to a trusted spiritual adviser to determine which tasks are acceptable and which are not. Ciarrocchi is then careful to ask his patient to do *only* those tasks deemed acceptable. The man described in chapter 5 whose religious obsessions were successfully treated with exposure therapy by Dr. Ciarrocchi proves that with this understanding and patient approach, exposure therapy can be effective, even for the strictly religious.

Other times however, even this understanding approach is not enough. Dr. Ciarrocchi notes that some patients still refuse or are unable to comply with exposure therapy, even after they have gotten permission from religious advisers. He notes that his successfully treated patient might have refused to do the prescribed exposure of looking at catalog pictures if he had an unshakable belief that lustful feelings would emerge during the experience and that they would be sinful.[5] As Dr. Ciarrocchi has found, such strict beliefs are:

> Usually transmitted by subgroups within religious traditions who teach the necessity of strict legalistic conformity to spiritual or moral values. These subgroups transmit ethical guidelines that exceed the received norms of the majority. For example, one community of Italian monks places stiff-bristled scrub brushes in the shower stalls so monks need not touch their genitals when washing. Another woman has accepted the view of her religious educators that sex is, in itself, inherently nasty and disgusting, even if permitted in marriage; when she has sex with her husband, she puts her Bible in the drawer so as to not mix religious and sexual images in her mind.[6]

What can be done to change such strongly held beliefs? How would an expert in religious obsessions such as Dr. Minichiello advise a patient who truly believes that he or she is going to be punished by God for his or her thoughts? "In the end," he says, "what you really have to do is to help the person straighten out their theology—and unfortunately most psychotherapists don't have that kind of training. Because of my background I can try to do it, but you have to be very careful about whom the patient asks for help. They should consult with someone they trust in their denomination who understands OCD and religious obsessions." If a religious leader who does not understand these kind of obsessions is consulted, and the patient hears *anything* from him that reinforces a belief in eternal damnation, this usually makes the belief stronger and more resistant to change.

Dr. Minichiello advises his Catholic patients with religious obsessions to visit their local Paulist Center, or a Newman Center at a college or university, for spiritual direction. There they will find highly educated priests who are ecumenical-minded and who have all been trained in the more liberal post–Vatican II theology. Jews with religious obsessions might try to talk to a Reform rabbi, since an Orthodox rabbi who was unfamiliar with obsessions could unknowingly reinforce an obsessional fear. Happily, in my experience, most religious advisers have been sensitive and understanding in dealing with patients with religious obsessions. Often it is useful for the therapist to speak with the adviser to answer any questions he or she may have about OCD.

Bad Thoughts in Other Religions

Why has this chapter focused on the religious obsessions of Christians? Because, based on my and Dr. Minichiello's experience, blasphemous thoughts and the fear that they will lead to eternal damnation are most common in Catholics taught a pre–Vatican II theology, and in evangelical Protestants.

Do Jews, followers of Islam, and members of other organized religions have religious obsessions like these? Yes, although they often take a different form. I once consulted on the case of an emaciated young Jewish man who was hospitalized and was being nourished through a nasal tube emptying directly into his stomach. Nothing was physically wrong with him. He had become so tormented, paralyzed, by attempting to comply perfectly with all the Jewish dietary laws that he had stopped eating altogether, despite being told by the chief rabbi in the United States that his fears were irrational. Some observant Jews do suffer from the bad thoughts that are the subject of this book. Drs. David Greenberg and Eliezer Witztum, of Herzog Hospital in Jerusalem, reported that of thirty-four referrals for OCD, nineteen were ultraorthodox Jews, and thirteen had religious obsessions.[7]

Do observant Jews sometimes get thoughts of eating pork in synagogue, or of defiling the Torah when the ark is opened, as the Imp of the Perverse would predict? I don't know. But I wouldn't be at all shocked if I met a patient with this problem.

In my experience, followers of Islam also tend to be troubled by fears of not performing religious rituals perfectly—such as not facing Mecca perfectly during prayer, or perhaps not praying at the correct time. Drs. Greenberg and Witztum describe the term *Waswas*, which, in a verse in the Koran, refers to evil thoughts or doubts preventing the proper completion of preprayer ritual washing.[8]

Finally, two early studies from primarily Protestant England reported a low prevalence of religious obsessions in patients with OCD: two of forty-one in one study,[9] and none of forty-five in the other.[10] Why are these rates so low? Greenberg and Witztum hypothesize that the lack of centrality of religion in everyday life in England may be responsible.[11] Likewise, on a recent visit to London I was told that the Maudsley Hospital OCD program in London is rarely referred people with religious or blasphemous obsessions.

Apparently, in religious bad thoughts, as with all others, the Imp of the Perverse operates in his usual way, tormenting the sufferer with bad thoughts of *doing whatever the surrounding culture considers the most inappropriate thing he or she could possibly do.* Since what is considered most inappropriate varies from culture to culture and religion to religion, so do the thoughts the imp seizes upon to cause his mischief.

8

Medications for Bad Thoughts

The desire to take medicine is perhaps the greatest feature
which distinguishes man from animals.
—Sir William Osler (1849–1919)

In the century since Dr. Osler's observation, medicines have been
discovered to ease many of mankind's ills, including the ills of the
mind: anxiety, depression, and frighteningly disorganized thinking. The psychiatrist who specializes in the treatment of mental problems with drugs is today called a psychopharmacologist,
and he, too, has something to tell us about treatments for bad
thoughts.

I devote this chapter primarily to the so-called serotonin-
reuptake inhibiting (SRI) drugs. No matter if the cause is OCD,
depression, PTSD, or Tourette's syndrome,[1] the SRI drugs are
those most commonly prescribed for, and offer the most promise
of helping, intrusive thoughts.

In theory, every mental health professional should agree that a
problem is preferably controlled by nondrug means. After all,
heart specialists such as Dr. Dean Ornish are far happier if changing my diet and exercise habits stops the blockage of my arteries
rather than an operation and then repeated trips to the phar-
macy.[2] So try the nondrug treatments for severe bad thoughts described in the previous chapters. If you are not satisfied with your
progress on your own, then by all means see a qualified mental

health professional who is familiar with these problems and treatment techniques. My experience is that you should expect relief from this nondrug approach—although the degree of improvement differs from person to person.

If, however, you find your bad thoughts do not respond to your hard work with nondrug treatments such as exposure therapy or cognitive therapy, then by all means consider consulting your physician or psychiatrist to see if a medication might give you relief. Your doctor will probably suggest you try one of the serotonin-reuptake inhibitor drugs, which are classified as antidepressants for their most frequent use. These drugs appear to work by making more of the brain neurotransmitter serotonin available to the nerve cells in our brains, thereby reducing a variety of obsessions, including some of the bad thoughts that are the subject of this book.

Many of the patients I described earlier had been taking an SRI drug when I saw them for treatment. Some, such as Frank—who couldn't feel certain that he wouldn't one day snap and become a serial killer like Jeffrey Dahmer—got little relief despite trying a number of these drugs at varying doses, over varying lengths of time. Others, like Ginny—the grandmother who was afraid of killing her grandchild while baby-sitting—swears that she would never have had the courage to confront her fears with exposure therapy with me had she not been taking an SRI drug. And still others, such as Martie, had other obsessions and compulsions besides her fear of harming her baby; she found that an SRI drug controlled these other OCD symptoms—checking door locks over and over again, for example—but did not help her bad thoughts about her son.

Over the past decade I have spoken to hundreds of patients who take SRI drugs, and I have worked on many studies of the usefulness of these drugs. However, as a psychologist—not a physician—I cannot prescribe these or any other drugs. Consequently, I have turned to two practicing psychiatrists with extensive experience in treating obsessions for their views about drug treatment of bad thoughts: Dr. Katherine Wisner, whose research on violent thoughts in women with postpartum depression I described earlier, and my longtime colleague and friend Dr. Michael

Jenike. I first consider the role of drug treatment for bad thoughts in general.

Medication Treatment for Bad Thoughts

We know that SRI drugs are effective against the obsessions of OCD in general, but what about violent, sexual, or blasphemous obsessions in particular? Apart from a few anecdotal reports in the literature, we know little about this question.

The only study to directly address the effectiveness of these drugs against sexual obsessions was carried out by Drs. Dan Stein and Eric Hollander at Mount Sinai Medical School in New York. They reviewed the charts of all their patients who had been treated with SRI drugs for a variety of sexual disorders and discovered that the greatest improvement was in those people with "ego-dystonic, intrusive sexual obsessions typical of OCD"[3]; in other words, they found that SRI drugs were effective against the type of sexual bad thoughts that are the subject of this book.

Concerning religious or blasphemous obsessions, Drs. Brian Fallon and Michael Liebowitz and their associates at Columbia University Medical School studied the effectiveness of SRI drugs in ten patients with "moral or religious scrupulosity."[4] They found that six of the ten patients responded by the end of three months of treatment, and two more responded after longer treatment trials.

Other than these reassuring findings, there are no studies specifically addressing whether medications help particular types of obsessions. On the other hand, Dr. Jenike points out that since these obsessions occur in many patients with OCD, these bad thoughts have been treated as part of all drug studies that have been conducted in OCD. "Because," Dr. Jenike says, "these studies have all found that SRI medications help obsessive thoughts as much as compulsive rituals, there really aren't any particular drugs that I would prescribe first for a patient with sexual, violent, or blasphemous obsessions as opposed to any other OCD symptom."

Which drugs help obsessions and how do we know they're effective?

Today we have six SRI drugs that have been shown to be useful in carefully done double-blind studies (in which neither the doctor nor patient knew whether the active drug or a placebo had been prescribed). This is the gold standard way of testing a new drug because its effectiveness can be evaluated in an unbiased way. These drugs are fluvoxamine (Luvox), fluoxetine (Prozac), sertraline (Zoloft), paroxetine (Paxil), citalopram (Celexa), and clomipramine (Anafranil). Anafranil has been around the longest and is the best studied around the world, but growing evidence suggests that the other SRI drugs are probably equally effective against obsessions.[5]

At what dosages are SRI drugs used to treat obsessions?

In Dr. Jenike's experience, most people with OCD require relatively high dosages of these drugs to get relief from obsessions. He suggests the following guidelines based on the studies done to date: Luvox (up to 300 mg/day), Prozac (40–80 mg/day), Zoloft (up to 200 mg/day), Paxil (40–60 mg/day), Celexa (up to 60 mg/day), Anafranil (up to 250 mg/day). On the other hand, Dr. Jenike has also seen a few patients who did not respond to even large dosages of these medications, but who did improve on very low doses (such as 5–10 mg/day of Prozac or 25 mg/day of Anafranil).

Why do the SRI drugs help obsessions?

We don't fully understand why these particular drugs help intrusive thoughts while similar drugs do not. But we do have some important clues: Each of these drugs has powerful effects on serotonin, a neurotransmitter, or chemical messenger, in the brain. Serotonin is one of several chemicals that nerve cells in many parts of our brain use to communicate with one another. Because the nerve cells that use serotonin are distributed widely throughout our brain, the neurotransmitter affects much of our mental life, including obsessive thoughts and depression.

How do SRI drugs work?

Although we don't fully understand the process, we do know that a nerve cell is active only when a neurotransmitter like serotonin is present in the gap between it and it's neighboring nerve cell in our brain (these gaps are called synapses or the synaptic cleft). A nerve cell stops transmitting information to its neighboring nerve cell when it reabsorbs its neurotransmitter from the synapse, ending the transmission. The anti-obsessional drugs are called serotonin reuptake inhibitors (or SRIs) because they work by slowing the reuptake (another word for reabsorption) of serotonin, thereby keeping it in the synapse longer, so transmission can continue between the neighboring nerve cells. After a few weeks, this increased serotonin produces changes in serotonin receptors on the surface of the nerve cells (areas where serotonin attaches). It may be that these receptors are abnormal in people with OCD, and that the changes that SRI drugs produce in them partly reverse OCD symptoms. "But," Dr. Jenike warns, "this is only part of how these drugs work; it is very likely that other brain chemicals in addition to serotonin are involved. For example, we know that when activity in the brain's serotonin system is changed, this also changes the activity of other brain systems."

If the explanation above confuses you, don't worry! Dr. Jenike reminds us that researchers themselves do not fully understand how these drugs work because it is all so complicated. But the good news is that we do know, after decades of research, how to treat patients, even though we do not know exactly why our treatments work.

How long do anti-obsessional drugs take to work?

Dr. Jenike always warns his patients—and their doctors, if they are not familiar with treating obsessions—not to give up on an SRI drug unless there has been no improvement despite taking it in a therapeutic dose for at least ten weeks. He has seen many patients who eventually responded well who felt no positive effects at all in the first few weeks of taking an SRI drug, experiencing only side effects. As a result some physicians give up too early on

SRI drugs, stopping after four to six weeks without a response, since this is the time needed for treatment of depression, with which they are more familiar. Precisely why SRI drugs take so long to work for obsessions remains a mystery.

Do SRI drugs have side effects?

Yes, SRI drugs, like all drugs, have side effects. And as with all drugs, the patient and his physician must weigh the benefits of the drug against the side effects. In Dr. Jenike's experience it is important for the patient to be open and forceful about any problems the medication may be causing. Sometimes simply changing the dosage or taking the drug at a different time of day fixes the problem.

These drugs commonly produce sexual side effects in both sexes—ranging from lowered sexual drive or delayed orgasm to total inability to have an erection or orgasm.[6] Although you may feel embarrassed to discuss these problems, it is important for you to tell your physician about them so that he or she can help you figure out how best to deal with them. Besides, these side effects are so common that your psychiatrist will not be surprised to hear about them.

Other common side effects of SRI drugs are nausea, inability to sit still, sleepiness, and too much energy. Weight gain can be a problem with SRI drugs, so a strict diet may be needed if your appetite is increased. Anafranil (which is structurally similar to the older, tricyclic antidepressants) may also cause drowsiness, dry mouth, racing heart, memory problems, concentration difficulties, and mainly in men, problems urinating. Despite this list of potential side effects, these drugs appear to be safe, even over many years, and all side effects disappear when the drugs are stopped.

Are there other drugs that might help my bad thoughts?

Sometimes, people with intense images accompanying their bad thoughts, or those with tics, do not respond to either the non-drug treatments described earlier or to the SRI drugs. In these cases, a psychiatrist may prescribe, in addition to the SRI drug, another medication—called a dopamine antagonist, or neuroleptic drug—that acts on dopamine, another brain neurotransmitter. The theory behind this is that both visual hallucinations—seeing things that aren't there—and tics, such as in Tourette's syndrome, can be caused by too much dopamine in the synapses of our brains. This causes particular nerve cells to overfire, sending too many signals to our muscles or to the visual areas of our brain—causing us extraneous movements or images.

These drugs are sometimes called antipsychotics, after their most common usage. Does being prescribed one of these drugs mean then that you are psychotic? No. Although at high doses these drugs are used to treat symptoms of psychotic illness such as intense auditory or visual hallucinations and bizarre delusions, they are now used at lower doses to treat tics and, in combination with SRI drugs, to treat vivid upsetting mental images. As an example of this latter use, one of my patients complained about clear, and upsetting, images of stabbing his mother and father. After a week or two of taking a low dose of a neuroleptic drug, he told me that his stabbing images, which had previously been as vibrant as "oil paintings," were now more like vague "pencil sketches," which were far easier to tolerate. After this improvement, he was more willing to engage in exposure therapy, which dramatically reduced his distress and avoidance.

On the other hand, most psychiatrists will add these neuroleptic drugs only for serious problems, and only when they are convinced that no other nondrug or drug treatment alone will help. Why? Because the older drugs in this category—such as haloperidol (Haldol), pimozide (Orap), thioridazine (Mellaril), trifluoperazine (Stelazine), and chlorpromazine (Thorazine)—can produce permanent neurological problems, such as trembling or tongue thrusting. Fortunately, patients such as the man with vivid violent thoughts described above now have available newer neuroleptic drugs—such as quetiapine (Seroquel), olanzapine (Xyprexia), and risperidone (Risperdal)—that seem to cause fewer of these irreversible neurological problems. Still, Dr. Jenike warns that these new neuroleptic drugs should not be used alone since they may worsen OCD symptoms when not taken along with an SRI drug.

Bad Thoughts in Postpartum Depression

Before the first SRI drugs clomipramine (Anafranil) and fluoxetine (Prozac) became available in the late 1980s and early 1990s, Dr. Wisner had noticed that when she used the older tricyclic antidepressants (such as amitriptyline)[7] to treat women with postpartum depression, some of their symptoms—depression, sleep and appetite disturbance—got much better, but their obsessional thoughts and anxiety weren't totally relieved. Then when she started treating these women with the newly available SRI drugs, she often noticed far better control of their obsessional thoughts and anxiety.

Because women with postpartum depression often suffer from troubling anxiety, Dr. Wisner begins with low doses of SRI drugs—perhaps half the usual recommended starting dose—to keep from further elevating their anxiety. Although most of her patients with postpartum depression respond well to SRI drugs, Dr. Wisner told me that some of the new mothers she sees do not respond fully to these drugs. Although they notice their obsessions become fewer and less intense, they still remain, though causing less interference. She finds that adding behavior therapy (as described in earlier chapters) can markedly improve these mothers' recoveries.

Anna, the new mother you met earlier who feared accidentally poisoning her son, provides a clear illustration of the combined use of SRI drugs and exposure therapy. Several weeks prior to seeing me, Anna had been so depressed, and so unable to care for herself or her son, that she and her husband feared she might commit suicide, and she voluntarily checked into a nearby psychiatric hospital. There, her doctor immediately prescribed an SRI drug, and within two weeks she began to feel better. Her mood gradually brightened, her energy began to return, and she no longer fell asleep wishing she would not awaken. Yet Anna knew she was still far from being ready to face taking care of her infant son. Simply the thought of touching him caused her panic, as she imagined poisoning him with botulism, salmonella, or even poison ivy.

By the time Anna was referred by her psychiatrist to see me for behavior therapy, she had been taking the SRI drug for about one month and told me she was feeling enough like her old self to be ready to tackle her obsessional thoughts about her son. One of the first things I did was to visit Anna at her home to accomplish two key goals: (1) to help her practice touching various "poisonous" (though really safe) areas around her house and yard and then handle her son, and (2) with Anna there, to explain to her family what exposure therapy involved, and to reassure them that she was no longer suicidal and they need not—and she did not want them to—"treat her with kid gloves." With hard work, Anna no longer avoided anything in her home, including her son, whom she now touched and cared for normally. Since Anna told me that despite her marked improvement, she still had bad thoughts about poisoning him, we decided to prepare the exposure audiotape I described previously, which after two weeks of use was so helpful to her in taming her remaining bad thoughts.

Anna's story has a happy ending. It has now been more than a year since she completed treatment at our clinic—which also included several home visits by one of our dedicated counselors to supervise her in rough practices—and she returns from time to time to show us how tall her son has grown, to report on her continued progress, and most recently, offering to speak to other new mothers with thoughts like she had to give them hope and encouragement. Her treatment is typical: (1) an SRI drug improved her mood, returned her energy, and eliminated suicidal thinking; (2) exposure to handling her baby after touching feared things around her house eliminated her avoidance of both; and (3) imagining her most feared obsessions without distraction drained them of their strength.

Who Should Prescribe Anti-Obsessional Drugs for Me?

Although any licensed physician can legally prescribe any of the drugs discussed above, it is best to look for a board-certified psychiatrist who understands obsessions and OCD, preferably one who is also a psychopharmacologist. If you are given a prescription for an anti-obsessional medication and it is effective, your doctor will probably suggest you remain on it for a minimum of six months to one year before trying to discontinue it, to reduce the chance of relapse. Unfortunately many obsessions often return when drugs are discontinued, although not in all cases. This is another good reason for first, or simultaneously, giving a fair try to the nondrug treatments described earlier.

9

A Plan of Action

In the long run men hit only what they aim at.
—Henry David Thoreau (1817–1862)

The twelfth-century philosopher Maimonides divided the troubles that befall man into three classes:[1]

(1) Those troubles that result from possessing a human body. As a physician, Maimonides knew that an inevitable consequence of having a body was proneness to occasional diseases and birth deformities. Yet Maimonides considered the evils of this class to be comparatively rare. Today we might include in this class those problems whose cures require medications or surgery.

(2) Those troubles that people cause to each other—such as wars and crimes. Though Maimonides believed these evils more widespread than the first class, he still considered them to be uncommon in everyday life. Cases of physical or sexual abuse by parents or spouses would fall into this category—evils that often result in post–traumatic stress disorder, which I described earlier.

(3) Those troubles that we bring upon ourselves by our own actions: "This is the largest class and is far more numerous than the second class, and it is especially of these evils that all men complain." Here we might include those problems we bring upon ourselves by social isolation, thought suppression, thinking ourselves

evil, and avoiding fearful situations—problems that can sometimes lead to the brink of suicide.

For Maimonides, all troubles other than those due to having a human body were all due to the same cause: man's lack of wisdom. Being a teacher, Maimonides remained optimistic that by learning and by reducing our ignorance, we would then reduce the evils we bring upon ourselves and others.

Having invoked Maimonides's name, I wonder what he would think were he to read the preceding chapters. I fear he might be shocked by the frankness of some of the examples I give, though as a physician he would surely have been exposed to strange symptoms in his travels. On the other hand, I hope he might approve of my intent—which is to reduce our ignorance about why we have bad thoughts (we might even say these are inescapable consequences of having a human body) and so reduce the torment my patients bring upon themselves (a trouble of the third class).

But nature does not give up her secrets easily, and I am the first to admit that our understanding of bad thoughts, and how best to treat them, is far from complete. After reading the preceding chapters you should now have about as complete an understanding as anyone of bad thoughts in general, and of your bad thoughts in particular.

Starting to Tame Your Bad Thoughts

To help you take the first step in a program to begin taming your bad thoughts, I have collected in table 14 all the kinds of bad thoughts that I have discussed in the previous chapters. Although many items on this list are very similar, they differ in specific details. I have chosen to be overly inclusive in listing these characteristics of bad thoughts because I've found that most people only identify with symptoms that very closely resemble those they experience.

I suggest that you now go through this list, marking each bad thought that troubles you. Next, you may want to rank-order the thoughts you have marked in terms of how much trouble each causes you. Simply write *1* next to the most troublesome thought, *2* next to the next-most troublesome, and so on. Doing this begins to organize your plan for taming these thoughts, which you can refer back to later as a reminder.

TABLE 14

INVENTORY OF BAD THOUGHTS (INCLUDING URGES, IMAGES, AND SITUATIONS AVOIDED)

(1) Thoughts about harming your baby

(2) Worrying about molesting your daughter

(3) Worrying about steering your automobile into an innocent pedestrian

(4) Worrying about pushing a commuter in front of an oncoming train

(5) Urges to jump from the top of a tall building

(6) Thoughts about harming an innocent child

(7) Urges to jump off a mountain

(8) Urges to jump in front of an oncoming train

(9) Urges to push another person in front of a train or automobile

(10) Unacceptable sexual thoughts about people you know

(11) Unacceptable sexual thoughts toward strangers

(12) Sexual thoughts toward religious figures such as God, Jesus, or Mary

(13) Incestuous thoughts or urges

(14) Worrying about saying racist things

(15) Worrying that deep down you're really a violent criminal

(16) Worrying that you'll kill your children the way Susan Smith did

(17) Worrying that you'll become a killer like Jeffrey Dahmer

(18) Worrying about throwing your baby against a wall

(19) Worrying about fracturing your baby's skull

(20) Worrying about smothering your baby with a pillow

(21) Worrying about stabbing your baby with a knife

(22) Worrying about molesting your baby while changing him

(23) Worrying that you'll one day snap and harm your baby

(24) Imagining a dog jumping in front of your car and being run over

(25) Worrying about swerving your car off the road

(26) Worrying about shouting obscenities in public

(27) Avoiding children for fear of harming them

(28) Avoiding TV shows, movies, books, and magazines because they trigger violent thoughts

(29) Avoiding television, movies, and magazines, because they trigger sexual thoughts

(30) Worrying about having sex with animals

(31) Worrying that you really want to have sex with animals

(32) Worrying about staring at a dog's genitals

(33) Thoughts about killing your children or spouse

(34) Worrying about being compelled by the devil to harm your family

(35) Thoughts of killing people while driving

(36) Worrying about throwing children off a bridge

(37) Worrying about poisoning your infant

(38) Thoughts of homosexual acts

(39) Thoughts of having sex with people you brush against

(40) Avoiding using knives

(41) Worrying you might be gay

(42) Worrying you might shout out racial slurs

(43) Worrying you would stare at women's breasts, buttocks, or crotch

(44) Worrying you would stare at men's crotch

(45) Incestuous sexual thoughts

(46) Worrying about being sexually aroused around your father or mother

(47) Worrying that while using a knife you might lose control and stab someone

(48) Worrying that you'll say things like "I hope your baby dies!"

(49) Worrying that you might smother a baby in his carriage by covering him with his blanket

(50) Avoiding looking at baby's genitals while changing him for fear of wanting to molest him

(51) Trying to convince yourself you haven't molested someone

(52) Obsessions about putting a baby in the microwave oven

(53) Obsessions about throwing a baby down a flight of stairs

(54) Images of a baby lying dead in a casket

(55) Images of baby bleeding and injured

(56) Images of baby being eaten by sharks

(57) Worrying you might drown a baby
(58) Worrying you'll engage in a mass shooting
(59) Worrying you committed some crime while asleep
(60) Worrying you committed some crime while intoxicated
(61) Worrying about running over pedestrians with your car
(62) Checking to make sure you haven't hurt a child
(63) Asking for reassurance that you haven't done something wrong
(64) Checking to make sure that you haven't shouted an insult
(65) Worrying about smashing a crucifix in church
(66) Worrying about committing blasphemous acts while in church
(67) Thoughts of violent acts in sex
(68) Thoughts of sexually punishing a loved one
(69) Thoughts of unnatural sex acts
(70) Thoughts of sex with animals
(71) Impulse to engage in sexual practices that cause pain to the partner
(72) Sexual impulses toward attractive females, known or unknown to you
(73) Impulses to sexually assault a female, known or unknown to you
(74) Blasphemous sexual images about the Virgin Mary or Jesus
(75) Thoughts of harming children or elderly people
(76) Imagining that someone close to you was hurt or harmed
(77) Impulse to violently attack and kill a dog
(78) Impulse to violently attack and kill someone
(79) Thinking or wishing that someone would disappear from the face of the earth
(80) Impulse to hit or harm someone
(81) Feelings of intense anger toward someone related to a past experience
(82) Impulse to harm children, especially smaller ones
(83) Impulse to shout at someone
(84) Impulse to attack certain persons
(85) Impulse to physically and verbally attack someone
(86) Impulse to attack and violently punish someone (such as to throw a child out of a bus)
(87) Impulse to say rude things to people

(88) Impulse to say something nasty and damning to someone
(89) Impulse to say inappropriate things (the "wrong thing in the wrong place" impulse)
(90) Impulse to say rude and unacceptable things
(91) Impulse to push people away or onto the ground
(92) Blasphemous thoughts during prayers
(93) Obsessions about brushing against others
(94) Avoiding crowd spaces because of fears of being accused of molesting others

Before you attempt *any* of the exposure tasks described in chapter 5, you must first make sure that this treatment is safe for you to carry out. Begin by rereading chapter 3, keeping in mind that the overwhelming majority of people with bad thoughts need have no concerns that they will ever act on their thoughts. Of course, if you have OCD and have trouble feeling certain, even though you have never acted in an impulsively violent or sexual way in the past; and even though you feel terribly guilty about your thoughts; and even though you do not feel suppressed hatred toward people who have done you wrong or bullied you; and even though you do not enjoy fantasizing about getting even with them; and even though you have no strong urges or a plan to kill or injure yourself—in other words, even though your bad thoughts are harmless—still you may not feel comfortable using the techniques described in the previous pages. If so, don't worry! If through the preceding pages you have learned enough about your bad thoughts for you to seek help from a mental health professional, then this book will have served its purpose.

On the other hand, if after reviewing chapter 3 you find real reasons for concern about the possibility of your acting on your thoughts, you should first speak to your doctor or clergyman or mental health professional. There are now effective treatments that can ensure that you never act on your thoughts—by intervening now, you can prevent a potentially dangerous situation later. Remember Maimonides's view: By gaining wisdom now, you may single-handedly reduce the evils we cause to one another later. This is praiseworthy, not something to be ashamed of!

To review once again the warning signs that you should watch out for, ask yourself the following questions:

- Do you hear voices or see things that other people don't see?
- Do you feel intense anger or fantasize about retaliating against people who have harmed you?
- Have you acted on your sexual or violent thoughts in the past toward animals or people (intoxicated or sober)?
- Do you have strong urges to harm or kill yourself?

If you answer yes to any of these questions, you should talk to someone, preferably a mental health professional, before using the exposure techniques described earlier. Even if you answered no to all the questions above (as most readers will), I still advise you to find *someone* with whom you feel comfortable discussing your bad thoughts. I know you've gone out of your way to avoid doing this for a long time, but it has two valuable benefits: (1) Talking to another person about your bad thoughts provides an exposure exercise for you, and (2) talking to another person about your bad thoughts lifts some of the burden of the shame and the guilt that you've been feeling. For example, in conducting support groups for people suffering from bad thoughts, I've seen firsthand that discussing their bad thoughts with others who understand and have similar problems lessens their burden. In some cases I've witnessed people who haven't made eye contact with others for years, staring only at the floor, now beginning to look others in the eye. If you can't speak to a family member, and you can't find a friend to speak to, then perhaps you might feel comfortable speaking to a clergyman.

If your bad thoughts touch on religious themes or blasphemy, carefully reread chapter 7. Then honestly examine your own conception of God. If your conception is of a retaliating, vindictive God, then you should speak to a moderate clergy member of your denomination who can help you clarify your theology before doing any exposure treatment.

Most importantly, always remember that *by trying to suppress your thoughts, you're not helping, and you may well be making your thoughts worse.* If you change nothing else after reading this book, please try to stop suppressing your bad thoughts and let them pass naturally through your mind. Many people have told me that this single change greatly reduced the distress their bad thoughts caused them.

If you do decide to engage in the kind of exposure tasks described in chapter 5, you should begin by making a list of all the situations that you can think of that you have been avoiding because of each of your bad thoughts. This list will then become your blueprint for an exposure therapy plan. You should go into these situations that trigger your bad thoughts, then remain in the situation, not leaving or distracting yourself as you normally would, and especially not trying to suppress your bad thoughts while you are there. Reread chapter 5 before doing this. Especially make sure that you understand how the process of habituation works. It is important for you to let habituation run its course for you to once again feel at ease in these situations.

If you find that your bad thoughts are usually triggered by your feeling angry, you would benefit from learning how to better control your anger. A variety of anger management courses are offered in both mental health settings and adult education classes.

If you find that exposure therapy triggers memories of traumatic events from your past, refer back to chapter 4 to read about post–traumatic stress disorder. If your bad thoughts are not getting better, and you think this might be part of the reason, I suggest you read Dr. Herman's book[2] as soon as possible, then find a mental health practitioner whom you feel you can trust and relate to.

If you decide to try audiotaped exposure therapy as described in chapter 5, you should begin by writing down in detail the very worst thing you can think might happen if you acted on your thoughts. Write it down on a sheet of paper, then go back and read it, crossing out any reassurances you've given yourself, then record this onto a cassette tape. Refer back to the examples I gave in chapter 5 of audiotape scripts that our patients have used successfully. Most people are able to record their script onto a thirty-second or a sixty-second endless-loop tape (these are sold by stores such as RadioShack for outgoing messages on telephone answering machines). Listen to this tape in a personal tape player for at least one hour a day, and whenever else the thoughts come during the day, listening until the thoughts stop. If your script runs for many minutes, you will have to record it onto one side of a standard thirty-, forty-five-, or sixty-minute cassette tape, recording the script over and over until a single side is filled. Then listen to this tape in your recorder and rewind it to continue your exposure.

Some patients tell me that thinking about or listening to their horrible scenes on tape seems to make them feel even more guilty. If you find that you are not improving with audiotape exposure, you can try the method suggested to me by Jonathan Ash and Chris Draycott, both nurse-clinicians in Dr. Isaac Marks's OCD Treatment Program at the Maudsley Hospital in London. They ask their patients to record in their own voice phrases such as "I *may or may not* kill a child" or "I *may or may not* hate God"— whatever phrase is appropriate. They explained to me that their patients often find this kind of endless audiotape acceptable because it provides exposure to the *doubt* they must learn to live with if they are to resume normal functioning. If this approach makes sense to you, by all means give it a try.

I strongly suggest that before doing exposure therapy, you read through the various cognitive therapy techniques covered in detail in chapter 6, to determine if any of the misinterpretations listed there are problems that you are currently having. If so, you should try to work (preferably along with someone you trust, but if this is impossible, alone) to identify your irrational thoughts, then set up experiments to test them, and if necessary, to change them to more closely match reality.

Research has proven that some people are able to use self-help techniques effectively for their problems, while others will require a mental health professional to help them along. If you suffer from severe bad thoughts, or your bad thoughts are accompanied by serious thoughts about suicide or planning for suicide, you should be working with a mental health professional. Because having bad thoughts probably qualifies you for a diagnosis of obsessive-compulsive disorder (even if you've never considered this diagnosis before), you can take advantage of this by contacting the O.C. Foundation to find a therapist in your area who has experience treating these problems. (O.C. Foundation, Inc., 337 Notch Hill Road, North Branford, CT 05471, Telephone (203) 315-2190; www.ocfoundation.org)

In table 15 I have listed what I consider to be the most important "take-home" points you should have after reading this book. It might be helpful for you to write these key points on an index card so you can carry it in your wallet or purse for easy and frequent reference when your bad thoughts come.

TABLE 15
KEY "TAKE-HOME" POINTS

---

(1) *Everyone* has sexual, violent, or blasphemous thoughts pass through their mind from time to time.
(2) At times we all think the *very most inappropriate thing possible.*
(3) These thoughts are part of human nature, and having these thoughts *does not make you a bad person.*
(4) The more you try to suppress these thoughts, the stronger the thoughts will become.
(5) The more you avoid situations that trigger your thoughts, the worse your problem will become.
(6) If you stop trying to suppress bad thoughts, they will eventually pass naturally through your mind.
(7) Your goal is not to be able to completely control your thoughts—no one can do this!

If you follow the procedures in the proceeding chapters, many of you will notice a reduction in your bad thoughts. Some of you, however, will also require a medication to better control your bad thoughts. If so, try to find a psychiatrist who is familiar with the SRI medications that are described in chapter 8, or call the OC Foundation for help with finding a psychiatrist in your area.

Assessing Your Progress

How should you assess your progress in taming your thoughts? As you know by now, the worst thing you can do is to set a goal of "never having another bad thought" or "completely controlling my thoughts"—these are impossible goals that will only make you more self-conscious and frustrated. Do not fall into this trap of perfectionism. Rather, I tell my patients a much better goal is to improve their overall quality of life.

In reality, quality of life is the single most important thing that we strive for—we all know people who have physical or mental handicaps or illnesses who nevertheless lead wonderful lives and have a high quality of life. Conversely, we also all know people with excellent health and plenty of money who have a low quality of life.

Because of this, my colleagues and I in the Department of Psychiatry at Massachusetts General Hospital have, over the past five years, been developing a brief rating scale that can help you keep track of changes in your quality of life. Over the years we have interviewed a large number of patients in our psychiatric clinics, asking them how they would want their lives to be if their treatment was successful. We have also interviewed a large number of psychologists, psychiatrists, neurologists, and neurosurgeons at our hospital, asking them what a positive outcome for their patients would look like. Although our patients come from many walks of life (and have a variety of psychiatric problems—large and small), and the doctors come from many different orientations (some doing traditional talk therapy, others prescribing medications, and others performing surgery), we have found definite common threads in what we identify as a good quality of life.

After a variety of statistical tests to reduce the number of items down to a manageable number, we ended up with ten items that did the job we were looking for. Table 16 contains the final ten-item scale, called the SOS-10.[3] Interestingly, we found that the single item that correlated most highly with overall quality of life was peace of mind—this should not come as a surprise to anyone suffering from bad thoughts! Please take a few moments now to complete the scale before you start working on your bad thoughts.

TABLE 16

QUALITY OF LIFE SCALE
(SOS-10 © 1997 BY MGH DEPARTMENT OF PSYCHIATRY)

Instructions: Below are ten statements about you and your life that help us see how you feel you are doing. Please respond to each statement by circling the response number that best fits how you have generally been over the last seven days (one week). There are no right or wrong responses, and it is important that your responses reflect how you feel you are doing. Often the first answer that comes to mind is best. Thank you for your thoughtful effort. Please be sure to respond to each statement.

(1) Given my current physical condition, I'm satisfied with what I can do.

Never   0   1   2   3   4   5   6   All the time
or nearly
all the time

(2) I have confidence in my ability to maintain important relationships.

Never   0   1   2   3   4   5   6   All the time
or nearly
all the time

(3) I feel hopeful about my future.

Never   0   1   2   3   4   5   6   All the time
or nearly
all the time

(4) I am often interested and excited about things in my life.

Never   0   1   2   3   4   5   6   All the time
or nearly
all the time

(5) I am able to have fun.

Never   0   1   2   3   4   5   6   All the time
or nearly
all the time

(6)   I'm generally satisfied with my psychological health.
Never   0   1   2   3   4   5   6   All the time
                                                  or nearly
                                                  all the time

(7)   I am able to forgive myself for my failures.
Never   0   1   2   3   4   5   6   All the time
                                                  or nearly
                                                  all the time

(8)   My life is progressing according to my expectations.
Never   0   1   2   3   4   5   6   All the time
                                                  or nearly
                                                  all the time

(9)   I am able to handle conflicts with others.
Never   0   1   2   3   4   5   6   All the time
                                                  or nearly
                                                  all the time

(10) I have peace of mind.
Never   0   1   2   3   4   5   6   All the time
                                                  or nearly
                                                  all the time

To calculate your total score, simply add your scores for each of the ten items (the total should be somewhere between 0 and 60). A higher score on the scale indicates a higher quality of life, or better overall psychological functioning. We found that improvements in scores on this scale provide a good measure of the improvement of our patients with successful treatment for their psychological problems.

If you would like to compare your score to those of others who have taken this scale, table 17 gives you the mean (or average) scores, and the range of scores for three groups of people we studied: (1) a group of inpatients in Massachusetts General Hospital psychiatry units, and those being evaluated in our psychiatric emergency room, (2) a group of outpatients in our psychiatry clinics, who were less ill than the inpatient group and for the most part were able to work or to go to school between sessions, and (3) a group of nonpatients who work at our hospital.

TABLE 17
SCORING RANGES FOR SOS-10 SCALE

Group	Average Score	Scoring Range
(1) Psychiatric inpatients/ER	29	16–42
(2) Psychiatric outpatients	37	32–42
(3) Nonpatients	45	41–49

As we would expect, group 1 had the lowest average score, followed by groups 2 and 3. However, as individuals in groups 1 and 2 improved, so did their scores on our scale.

By tracking your progress with a quality-of-life scale such as this, you'll keep your focus squarely on something that you can control. Since you can never control your thoughts completely, the next best thing is to let them pass through your mind and not attempt to suppress them. The goal is to reach a point where the thoughts no longer torment you, and where you do not torment yourself when they do come from time to time. Most of all, your goal should be to have as high a quality of life as possible, along with peace of mind.

Conclusion

So where in the end will we find our Imp of the Perverse? Is he hiding in our genes, dictating which proteins to produce and when? Or is he lurking in the soup filling the synapses between our brain's nerve cells, ever ready to send flurries of electrical charges to terrify us? Perhaps our culture nurtures and feeds him, giving him his power by its warnings to suppress our bad thoughts lest we risk ostracism in this life, or damnation in the one to follow. Or perhaps particularly hospitable living conditions are laid down for him in some of us in the earliest months of life, when some of our nervous systems are tuned to an exquisite sensitivity to warn us of perceived threats. Is he found in the flood of hormones circulating in the blood of new mothers, coaxing them to be overly aware of any dangers to their new baby? Or perhaps, it is best after all to consider him—to use Maimonides's words—a necessary trouble that comes along with having a human body.

As modern neuroscience progresses, we are struck by the incredible complexity of our brains and nervous systems. We recognize more clearly all the time the complex and changeable network of structural and functional units that blur the ancient mind-body distinction to the point of irrelevance. Simple cause-and-effect answers are too much to ask for where human behavior is concerned.

Our search for the Imp of the Perverse reminds me of surgeon and essayist Richard Selzer's fanciful goal of one day, deep in the entrails of one of his patients, finally holding in his gloved hand the mysterious organ responsible for love sickness:

> Thus I have engaged in the initial hypothesis (call it a hunch) that there is somewhere in the body, under the kneecap perhaps, or between the fourth and fifth toes . . . somewhere . . . a single, as yet unnoticed master gland, the removal of which would render the person so operated upon immune to love. Daily in my surgery, I hunt this *glans amoris*, turning over membranes, reaching into dim tunnels, straining all the warm extrusions of the body for some residue that will point the way. Perhaps I shall not find it in my lifetime. But never, I vow it, shall I cease from these labors, and shall charge those who come after me to carry on the search. Until then I would agree with my uncle Frank, who recommends a cold shower and three laps around the block for the immediate relief of the discomforts of love.[4]

Like the search for the ultimate site of lovesickness, the search for the Imp of the Perverse is far off, hopelessly mixed up with the rest of what makes us human. But when the bad thoughts, which are the imp's calling card, become more than mere nuisance and cause us pain, some concrete steps—slightly more complex than Uncle Frank's prescription—can help tame these thoughts. In the preceding chapters, I have tried to lay out the most current thinking on the causes and treatment of violent, sexual, and religious bad thoughts. If you follow the instructions given here, most of you will find some measure of relief from your bad thoughts. I wish you the best of luck in your efforts. Now, if only those dogs would keep out of those pickup truck beds . . .

Notes

PREFACE

1. Michael A. Jenike, Lee Baer, and William E. Minichiello, eds., *Obsessive-Compulsive Disorders: Practical Management*, 3rd. ed. (St. Louis: Mosby, 1998).
2. Lee Baer, *Getting Control: Overcoming Your Obsessions and Compulsions*, rev. ed. (New York: Plume, 2000).

CHAPTER 1

1. We are just beginning to learn what factors determine the outcome for a particular person. It appears that the way we react to the thoughts, and whether we are suffering from obsessive-compulsive disorder or depression when the thoughts occur, are key factors, as will be discussed later.
2. *Melancholy* was a term used to describe the condition we now call depression.
3. And not coincidentally, it appears that people who are the most conscientious, and sensitive to other people thinking well of them, may be the most prone to suffer from severe bad thoughts.
4. A major problem for people suffering from obsessive-compulsive disorder is that, no matter how hard they try, they cannot achieve a feel-

ing of certainty in many situations. Hence, like Isaac, they are tormented by doubt.

5. Isaac told me that he had a vivid memory of an elementary-school classmate who was teased unmercifully by the other boys because of an unfounded rumor that he had had intercourse with a pet cat.

6. Lee Baer, *Getting Control: Overcoming Your Obsessions and Compulsions*, rev. ed. (New York: Plume, 2000).

7. The YBOCS is the gold standard measure of obsessive-compulsive disorder symptoms, and its ten questions yield a total score between zero and forty, with sixteen indicating clinically significant OCD symptoms.

8. Father Jack's case was less helpful for our study, since treatment responders in the placebo group make it less likely that the active drug will be found to be significantly more effective than the placebo. I must admit I didn't lose any sleep over this problem however.

9. Significantly, sufferers of both depression and obsessive-compulsive disorder tend to see things as either black or white, with no gray in between—in the way Dr. Jekyll saw the "moral" and "wicked" parts of his personality as polar opposites, rather than as part of a continuum with mixtures in between. Jekyll indeed suggests significant obsessional tendencies in himself with the lines: "And indeed, the worst of my faults was a certain impatient gaiety of disposition, such as has made the happiness of many, but such as I found it hard to reconcile with my imperious desire to carry my head high, and wear a more than commonly grave countenance before the public. Hence it came about that I concealed my pleasures; and that when I reached years of reflection, and began to look round me and take stock of my progress and position in the world, I stood already committed to a profound duplicity of life. Many a man would have even blazoned such irregularities as I was guilty of; but from the high views that I had set before me, I regarded and hid them with an almost morbid sense of shame. It was thus rather the exacting nature of my aspirations, than any particular degradation in my faults, that made me what I was and, with even a deeper trench than in the majority of men, severed in me those provinces of good and ill which divide and compound man's dual nature."

CHAPTER 2

1. C. T. Beck, "The Lived Experience of Postpartum Depression: A Phenomenological Study," *Nursing Research* 41 (1992): 166–70.

2. The study included sixty-five women between the ages of eighteen and forty-five who had come to the Women's Mood Disorder Clinic

suffering from major depression, but who did not suffer from obsessive-compulsive disorder before the birth of their child. Of these women, thirty-seven had depression that began within three months of the birth of their child and were called the Postpartum Onset group (Dr. Wisner explains that she used three months rather than the usual four weeks as a cutoff for postpartum depression because the three-month time frame has better scientific support from epidemiological studies). The other twenty-eight women met the criteria for major depression but not within three months of childbirth, and so they were called the Non-Postpartum Onset group. All the women in both groups filled out the YBOCS Symptom Checklist from my book, and their answers were reviewed with them by Dr. Wisner.

When the results were analyzed, the researchers found that significantly more women with postpartum onset admitted to having aggressive thoughts (twenty out of thirty-seven, or 54%) than those with nonpostpartum onset (six out of twenty-eight, or 21%). As important, the specific obsessions reported by these women were almost always bad thoughts about harming their infants. Katherine L. Wisner, Kathleen S. Peindl, Thomas Gigliotti, and Barbara Hanusa, "Obsessions and Compulsions in Women with Postpartum Depression," *Journal of Clinical Psychiatry* 60 (1999): 176–80. Earlier my colleagues at Massachusetts General Hospital Perinatal Psychiatry Unit noted this constellation of symptoms in fifteen women. D. A. Sichel, L. S. Cohen, J. A. Dimmock, and J. F. Rosenbaum, "Postpartum Obsessive Compulsive Disorder: A Case Series," *Journal of Clinical Psychiatry* 54 (1993): 156–59.

3. Wisner, Peindl, Gigliotti, and Hanusa, "Obsessions and Compulsions in Women with Postpartum Depression."
4. K. D. Jennings, S. Ross, S. Popper, and M. Elmore, "Thoughts of Harming Infants in Depressed and Nondepressed Mothers," *Journal of Affective Disorders* 54 (1999): 21–28.
5. A. D. Filer and I. F. Brockington, "Maternal Obsessions of Child Sexual Abuse," *Psychopathology* 29 (1996): 135–38.

CHAPTER 3

1. *Boston Herald*, September 28, 1999.
2. *Sports Illustrated*, September 13, 1999.
3. Lyall Watson, *Dark Nature: A Natural History of Evil* (New York: HarperCollins, 1997).
4. When I try to predict whether a person (usually a male, since males commit most violent crimes) is likely to commit a violent act in the

future, the best place to look is their past behavior. Those who commit violent acts as adults often have a history of acting violently in the past. When younger, they'll often have shown cruelty to animals or violence to other children. Although some individuals I've seen have been violent *only* while under the influence of alcohol or drugs, the fact that they have been violent in the past causes me to worry that they will one day act violently again. So when a patient asks me how I can be certain he won't act on his thoughts and urges, I point out that his never having acted on these thoughts and urges in the past is an excellent predictor that he will not act on them in the future.

5. Exposure therapy is an effective nondrug treatment for bad thoughts that is described in detail in chapter 5.

CHAPTER 4

1. Randy Thornhill and Craig T. Palmer, *A Natural History of Rape: Biological Bases of Sexual Coercion* (Cambridge, Mass.: MIT Press, 2000).

2. Lyall Watson, *Dark Nature: A Natural History of Evil* (New York: HarperCollins, 1997).

3. Ibid. In the United States, forty-three percent of all children so badly abused that they died were living at the time with stepparents. And in England, an astonishing fifty-two percent of all babies killed were beaten to death by stepfathers. Data for Canada, which also take the child's age into account, show that lethal "death by battering" is sixty-five times more likely to take place in a home that includes a new stepfather.

4. Ibid.

5. For those interested in learning more about this fascinating and controversial way of trying to understand puzzling human behaviors and problems, *Why We Get Sick: The New Science of Darwinian Medicine* by Drs. Randolph Nesse and George Williams (New York: Times Books, 1994) is required reading. In explaining possible evolutionary reasons for the physical and mental illnesses to which we fall prey, the authors, a respected psychiatrist and an eminent evolutionary theorist, provide wonderfully clear explanations of this new field of Darwinian medicine (named in honor of evolutionary pioneer Charles Darwin).

6. Daniel M. Wegner, *White Bears and Other Unwanted Thoughts: Suppression, Obsession, and the Psychology of Mental Control* (New York: Guilford Press, 1994).

7. K. D. Jennings, S. Ross, S. Popper, and M. Elmore, "Thoughts of

Harming Infants in Depressed and Nondepressed Mothers," *Journal of Affective Disorders* 54 (1999): 21–28.

8. H. Weightman, B. M. Dalal, and I. F. Brockington, "Pathological Fear of Cot Death," *Psychopathology* 31 (1998): 246–49.

9. American Psychiatric Association, *Diagnostic and Statistical Manual of Mental Disorders*, 4th ed. (Washington, D.C.: American Psychiatric Association, 1994).

10. This story appeared in an article by my colleague Steven C. Schlozman at Massachusetts General Hospital and McLean Hospital, entitled "Fits and Starts," *The Sciences*, November/December 1999, 38–42.

11. Oliver Sacks, *An Anthropologist on Mars: Seven Paradoxical Tales* (New York: Knopf, 1995), 91.

12. Ibid., 95.

13. J. F. Leckman, D. E. Grice, L. C. Barr, A. L. de Vries, C. Martin, D. J. Cohen, C. J. McDougle, W. K. Goodman, and S. A. Rasmussen, "Tic-Related vs. Non-Tic-Related Obsessive-Compulsive Disorder," *Anxiety* 1 (1994–95): 208–15.

14. A. H. Zohar, D. L. Pauls, G. Ratzoni, A. Apter, A. Dycian, M. Binder, R. King, J. F. Leckman, S. Kron, and D. J. Cohen, "Obsessive-Compulsive Disorder With and Without Tics in an Epidemiologic Sample of Adolescents," *American Journal of Psychiatry* 154 (1997): 274–76.

15. Lowell Handler, *Twitch and Shout* (New York: Plume, 1999).

16. Judith Herman, *Trauma and Recovery: The Aftermath of Violence—from Domestic Abuse to Political Terror* (New York: Basic Books, 1997), 121.

17. Ibid., 37.

18. This treatment technique is described in detail in chapter 5.

19. Exposure therapy and its guiding principle of habituation are described in chapter 5.

20. Elaine Aron, *The Highly Sensitive Person* (New York: Broadway Books, 1997), 10–11.

21. Jerome Kagan, *Galen's Prophecy* (New York: Basic Books, 1998), 238.

CHAPTER 5

1. Lee Baer, *Getting Control: Overcoming Your Obsessions and Compulsions*, rev. ed. (New York: Plume, 2000), 35–36.

2. *Desensitization* and *extinction* are technical terms that are often used interchangeably with *habituation*.

3. J. W. Ciarrocchi, "Religion, Scrupulosity, and Obsessive-Compulsive

Disorder," chapter 24 in M. A. Jenike, L. Baer, and W. E. Minichiello, eds., *Obsessive-Compulsive Disorders: Practical Management*, 3rd ed. (St. Louis: Mosby, 1998).

4. My colleague Dr. Isaac Marks in London has found that before recording an audiotape for exposure it is essential to make sure the script does not contain any phrases that might act as mental rituals (that is, that might artificially reduce distress). He found that before he eliminated these phrases from his patients' scripts, they obtained mixed results using these audiotapes for exposure. But after he began to preview these scripts and to cross out any mental rituals, he found improvement in patients' success rates. (K. Lovell, I. M. Marks, H. Noshirvani, and G. O'Sullivan: "Should Treatment Distinguish Anxiogenic from Anxiolytic Obsessive-Compulsive Ruminations?" *Psychotherapy Psychosomatics* 61 (1994): 150–55.)

5. This case is described in my book *Getting Control*.

6. Thanks to my colleagues Drs. Nancy Keuthen and Deborah Osgood-Hynes for providing these examples.

CHAPTER 6

1. For an easily understandable explanation of cognitive therapy as it is used to treat depression, see David Burns, *Feeling Good: The New Mood Therapy* (Maryland and New York: Morrow, 1980).

2. Much of the material in this section is modified from an article by Dr. Sabine Wilhelm entitled "Cognitive Therapy for Obsessive-Compulsive Disorder," in press in the *Journal of Cognitive Psychotherapy* 14 (2000): 43, and from her chapter of the same title in press in W. J. Lyddon, J. V. Jones, eds., *Empirically-Supported Cognitive and Cognitive Behavioral Strategies* (Springer).

3. This technique was introduced by David Burns in *Feeling Good*.

4. J. S. Beck, *Cognitive Therapy: Basics and Beyond* (New York: Guilford Press, 1995).

5. The chance of *all* of a series of events happening is found by multiplying together the chances of each event's happening individually. For example, the chance of flipping a coin and getting five heads in row is 1 in 32. Since the chance of each coin flip coming up heads is 1 in 2, the chance of *all* the five flips coming up heads is $\frac{1}{2} \times \frac{1}{2} \times \frac{1}{2} \times \frac{1}{2} \times \frac{1}{2}$, or $\frac{1}{32}$. If you prefer to work with probabilities rather than fractions, the solution is $.5 \times .5 \times .5 \times .5 \times .5$, or $.03125$, which equals $\frac{1}{32}$.

144   *Notes*

CHAPTER 7

1.Erik H. Erickson, *Young Man Luther: A Study in Psychoanalysis and History* (New York: W. W. Norton, 1962).

2. Joseph W. Ciarrocchi, "Religion, Scrupulosity, and Obsessive-Compulsive Disorder," in Michael A. Jenike, Lee Baer, and William A. Minichiello, eds., *Obsessive-Compulsive Disorders: Practical Management*, 3rd ed. (St. Louis: Mosby, 1998).

3. J. Moore, "Of Religious Melancholy," in D. Hunter and I. Macalpine, eds., *Three Hundred Years of Psychiatry, 1535–1860* (Cambridge: Cambridge University, 1963), 252–53.

4. Ciarrocchi, "Religion, Scrupulosity, and Obsessive-Compulsive Disorder."

5. Ibid.

6. Ibid.

7. D. Greenberg and E. Witztum, "Cultural Aspects of Obsessive-Compulsive Disorder," chapter 2 in E. Hollander, J. Zohar, D. Marazziti, and B. Olivier, eds., *Current Insights in Obsessive-Compulsive Disorder* (New York: Wiley, 1994).

8. Ibid.

9. J. H. Dowson, "The Phenomenology of Severe Obsessive-Compulsive Neurosis," *British Journal of Psychiatry* 131 (1977): 75–78.

10. R. S. Stern and J. P. Cobb, "Phenomenology of Obsessive-Compulsive Neurosis," *British Journal of Psychiatry* 132 (1978): 233–39.

11. Greenberg and Witztum, "Cultural Aspects of Obsessive-Compulsive Disorder."

CHAPTER 8

1. In Tourette's syndrome, the tics and twitches require treatment with drugs that affect dopamine rather than serotonin. However, the *obsessions* in Tourette's syndrome are thought to respond to SRI drugs that affect serotonin.

2. See *Dr. Dean Ornish's Program for Reversing Heart Disease.*

3. D. J. Stein, E. Hollander, D. T. Anthony et al., "Serotonergic Medications for Sexual Obsessions, Sexual Addictions, and Paraphilias," *Journal of Clinical Psychiatry* 53 (1992): 267–71. Ego-dystonic means these thoughts were unwanted and experienced as unpleasant.

4. B. A. Fallon, M. R. Liebowitz, E. Hollander et al., "The Pharmacotherapy of Moral or Religious Scrupulosity," *Journal of Clinical Psychiatry* 51 (1990): 517–21.

5. If you are interested in getting more information about the use of medications for treating OCD in general, and bad thoughts in particular, you can contact the O. C. Foundation to receive Dr. Jenike's pamphlet "Drug Treatment of OCD in Adults." Their phone number is (203) 315-2190, and their Web site is www.ocfoundation.org

6. An unusual side effect that has been reported is the occurrence of spontaneous orgasms while yawning! Dr. Jenike notes that this must be quite uncommon indeed, since none of his patients have ever reported this symptom and, to his knowledge, when they yawn in his office, the only emotion they feel is boredom. He has also found the occasional patient who complains of *increased* sexual interest while on SRI drugs.

7. Tricyclic antidepressants got their name from their chemical structure, which has three rings. Technically, clomipramine is considered a tricyclic antidepressant because of its chemical structure, although one of its action is to make more serotonin available in the brain, making it functionally an SRI drug. The newer SRI drugs, fluoxetine (Prozac), fluvoxamine (Luvox), paroxetine (Paxil), sertraline (Zoloft), and citalopram (Celexa), do not have a tricyclic chemical structure, and in addition, they target serotonin even more specifically than does clomipramine. As a result, the latter drugs are often referred to as selective serotonin-reuptake inhibitors, or SSRIs.

CHAPTER 9

1. Moses Maimonides, *The Guide for the Perplexed*, 2nd ed. (1904; reprint, New York: Dover, 1956).

2. Judith Herman, *Trauma and Recovery: The Aftermath of Violence from Domestic Abuse to Political Terror*.

3. M. A. Blais, W. R. Lenderking, L. Baer et al., "Development and Initial Validation of a Brief Mental Health Outcome Measure," *Journal of Personality Assessment* 73 (1999): 359–73.

4. R. Selzer, "Love Sick," chapter in *Confessions of a Knife* (New York: Touchstone, 1981), 114–15.

Index

Aggressive or violent thoughts, inappropriate, xiv, 5
 case studies, 33–34, 78–81
 exposure therapy for, 78–81, 88
Alcohol, 60–61
 effects on frontal cortex, 60
 thought suppression with, 12, 17
American Psychiatric Association, 36
Amitriptyline (Elavil), 120
Anafranil (clomipramine), 116, 118, 120
Anatomy of Melancholy, The (Burton), 106
Anger:
 management, 130
 as warning sign, 38–39, 44, 129
Animals, thoughts of sex with, 6, 11, 48
 exposure therapy for, 88–89
Antipsychotics, 119

Antisocial Personality Disorder, 39
 characteristics of, 40
Anxiety, 120
Aron, Elaine, 68
Ash, Jonathan, 131
Assessing your progress, 132–36
Audiotapes and videotapes
 used in exposure therapy, 80–86, 88–89, 104, 121, 130–31
Automobiles:
 fears of hitting pedestrians, xvi, 42
 urges to ruin the car, 55
Avoiding situations that trigger bad thoughts, xv, 6, 15, 42, 81, 93, 98

Bad thoughts:
 about harming children, see Children, thoughts of harming

aggressive, *see* Aggressive or
    violent thoughts,
    inappropriate
causes of, *see* Causes of bad
    thoughts
of clinical severity, 5
cognitive errors of OCD
    sufferers, 93–95
defined, xiv
fear of acting on, xv
during good times, 24–25
historical references to, 8–9,
    106
individual vulnerabilities and,
    9–11
inventory of, 125–28
numbers of people suffering
    from, xvii
paying little attention to, 6
relapses, 98–99, 122
religious, *see* Religious
    thoughts, blasphemous
secrecy about, *see* Secrecy
    about bad thoughts
sexual, *see* Sexual thoughts,
    inappropriate
statistics on, *see* Statistics
suicidal thoughts distinguished
    from, 52–53
suppressing, *see* Thought
    suppression
"take-home" points, 132
treatment of, *see* Treatment
uncertainty about acting on,
    see Uncertainty about acting
    on bad thoughts
universality of, 6–7, 8, 98
warning signs of dangerous
    behavior, 37–44, 128–29
Beck, Aaron, 91
Behavior therapy, *see* Exposure
    therapy
Brain:
    caudate nucleus, 59

cingulum, 59
complexity of the, 137
exposure therapy, effects of, 74
imaging, 59
limbic system, *see* Limbic
    system
neurotransmitters, *see*
    Neurotransmitters
orbital-frontal cortex, *see*
    Orbital-frontal cortex
Brockington, I. F., 28
Burton, Robert, 106

Carter, Jimmy, 17–18
Case studies, *see specific types of
    bad thoughts and treatments*
Causes of bad thoughts, 45–51
    evolutionary theories, 45–48
    Freudian theory, 48–49
    thought suppression, 49–51
Celexa (citalopram), 116
Child molestation, 31–32, 61,
    65–66
Child murderers, 31, 46
    Susan Smith, xv, 21, 32–33,
        41–42, 46
Children, Conduct Disorder in,
    see Conduct Disorder
Children, thoughts of harming,
    xvi, 19–30, 51
    case studies, xiii–xiv, 19,
        23–24, 25–27, 29–30, 41, 48,
        59, 120–21
    depression after postpartum
        period, 23–25
    evolutionary explanation for,
        47
    exposure therapy tasks, 86
    of grandmothers, 25–26
    men's, xvi, 28–30
    during postpartum depression,
        20–23
    postpartum psychosis and,
        42–43

Children *(cont'd)*
  sexual obsessions, 27–30
  statistics on, xvi, 22, 23–24
  teenagers, 24–25
Chlorpromazine (Thorazine),
  119
Ciarrocchi, Joseph, 76, 109–10
Citalopram (Celexa), 116
Clomipramine (Anafranil), 116,
  118, 120
Coaches, child molestation by,
  31–32
Cognitive therapy, 89, 108, 131
  alternatives to, *see* Exposure
    therapy; Medications
  assessing advantages and
    disadvantages of bad
    thoughts, 100
  behavioral experiments, 101–2
  calculating the true probability
    of danger, 102–3
  cognitive continuum
    technique, 102
  cognitive errors of OCD
    sufferers, 93–95
  combined with exposure
    therapy, 104–5
  for depression, 91
  "downward arrow" technique,
    100
  education about how thoughts
    and emotions work, 99–100
  logic behind, 91
  outcome of treatment with,
    103
  questioning basic beliefs, 102
  relapses, dealing with, 98–99
  self-administered, 105
  for sexual obsessions, 95–105
  Socratic questioning technique
    used in, 98
  theory behind treating
    obsessions with, 92–93, 97
  thought record, 98

thought suppression
  experiment, 99
College students, common bad
  thoughts in healthy, 7–8
Columbia University Medical
  School, 115
Columbine High School,
  shootings at, 32, 38–39, 44
Conduct Disorder, 39
  characteristics of, 40
Conscientious, being highly, 40,
  41, 57, 68

Dahmer, Jeffrey, xv, 33, 34, 42, 81
Danger, overestimating, 94
Dark Nature (Watson), 32–33
Depression, xiv
  clinical, 51–53
  cognitive therapy for, 91
  fears of harming children after
    postpartum period, 23–25
  postpartum, *see* Postpartum
    depression
Displacement, 66
Door locks, checking, xvi, xvii
Dopamine, 119
Dopamine antagonists, 119
Double-blind studies, 116
"Downward arrow" technique of
  cognitive therapy, 100
Draycott, Chris, 131
Driving:
  fears of hitting pedestrians, xvi,
    42
  urges to ruin the car, 55
Drugs:
  prescription, *see* Medications
  thought suppression with
    illegal, 12, 17

Emmelkamp, Paul, 91
Episodic memory, 61
Ethical issues, being overly
  conscientious about, 40, 41, 57

Evangelical Protestants, 111
Eve, biblical story of, 8
Evil, believing you are truly, 16–17
Evolutionary theories of bad
    thoughts, 45–48
Exposure therapy, 13–14, 34,
    63–90, 103
  alternative treatment, *see*
    Cognitive therapy;
    Medications
  audiotapes and videotapes
    used in, 80–86, 88–89, 104,
    121, 130–31
  brain chemistry changes
    resulting from, 74
  case studies, 76–86
  combined with cognitive
    therapy, 104–5
  expectations of, 86
  habituation as basis for, 74–76,
    79, 130
  help from others for, 90
  imaginal, 76
  in vivo, 76–81
  for obsessions about becoming
    homosexual, 87
  for obsessions about incest, 87,
    89
  for postpartum depression,
    120–21
  for post-traumatic stress
    disorder "memories," 66
  principles of, 73
  refusal to try, 89, 104
  for religious obsessions, 87, 88,
    106–11
  self-administered, 89–90,
    128–29, 130–31
  for sexual obsessions, 76–78,
    87, 88–89
  for thoughts of harming
    children, 86
  for violent obsessions, 78–81, 88
  in vivo, 86–87

Fallon, Brian, 115
Fear of acting on bad thoughts,
    xv
Filer, A. D., 28
Flashback memories:
  as symptoms of PTSD, 64
  distinction from obsessions,
    66–67
Fluoxetine (Prozac), 116, 120
Fluvoxamine (Luvox), 116
Freud, Sigmund, 30, 48–49, 62,
    66

Galen's Prophecy (Kagan), 68
*Getting Control: Overcoming Your
    Obsessions and Compulsions*
    (Baer), xvi, 20, 75–76
Grandchildren, thoughts of
    harming, 25–26
Greek myth of Pandora, 8
Greenberg, David, 112
Guilt, 42, 95, 129
  brain anatomy and, 41
  lack of, 38, 39, 42, 43
  as sign of never acting on bad
    thoughts, xiv, xvi, 30, 37, 39,
    40, 41

Habituation, 74–76, 79, 130
Hallucinations, 44, 119, 129
  visual images resembling,
    61–62
Haloperidol (Haldol), 119
Handler, Lowell, 60
Hand washing, xvi, xvii
Harvard Medical School, 57
Hebrew University, Israel, 55
Herman, Judith, 64, 65, 130
Herzog Hospital, Jerusalem, 112
Highly sensitive people, 67–69,
    108
Highly Sensitive Person, The
    (Aron), 67–68
Hollander, Eric, 115

Homosexuality:
  exposure therapy for obsessions
    about becoming gay, 87
  fear of, 10–11
Humor, 49

Id, 49, 62
Ignatius, St., 106
Implicit learning, 58
Imp of the Perverse:
  as literary simile, 3
  defined, 8
  historical examples of, 8–9
  Poe's description of, 3–4, 45
  search for the, 137
  thoughts chosen by, 9–10, 60,
    112
"Imp of the Perverse, The," 3–4
Inappropriate behavior at
    inappropriate times,
    thoughts of, *see* Bad
    thoughts
Incest:
  case example of fear of, 95–104
  cognitive therapy for
    obsessions about, 95–105
  exposure therapy for obsessions
    about, 87, 89
Infanticide, evolutionary theory
    for, 46
Infants, *see* Children, thoughts of
    harming
Introversion, 68
Inventory of bad thoughts,
    125–28
  using the, 124–28
Islam, followers of, 111, 112

Janet, Pierre, 5
Jenike, Michael, xvi, 114–19
Jennings, K. D., 23, 51
Jews with blasphemous thoughts,
    111, 112
Jung, Carl, 68

Kagan, Jerome, 68
Kosslyn, Stephen, 62

Leckman, James, 55
Liebowitz, Michael, 115
Limbic system, 59, 60, 61, 62
Luther, Martin, 106
Luvox (fluvoxamine), 116

McLean Hospital, xvii, 5
Maimonides, 123–24, 128, 136
Manson, Charles, 81
Marks, Isaac, 74, 131
Massachusetts General Hospital,
    xvi, 57, 92, 106, 133
  quality-of-life scale, 133–36
Mass murderers:
  Jeffrey Dahmer, *see* Dahmer,
    Jeffrey
  fear of becoming, 33, 34
Maudsley Hospital, London, 74,
    131
Media, fears instilled by the,
    31–32
Medications, 113–22, 132
  dopamine antagonists, 119
  dosages of SRIs, 116
  double-blind studies, 116
  how SRIs work, 116–17
  for obsessive-compulsive
    disorder, 13, 14, 113–22
  postpartum depression, for bad
    thoughts in, 120–21
  prescribers of, 121–22
  serotonin-reuptake inhibiting
    (SRIs), 113–18
  side effects of, 118, 119
  time until SRIs help, 117–18
  trying nondrug treatments first,
    113–14, 122
  see also specific medications
Mellaril (thioridazine), 119
Memory:
  episodic, 61

of OCD sufferers, 58
post-traumatic stress disorder
and, 62, 66, 130
Mental health professionals, seeking
help from, 89, 90, 113–14,
121–22, 128, 129, 131–32
locating a therapist, 131–32
Minichiello, William, xvi, 106–9,
111
Moore, John, 106
Moral issues, being overly
conscientious about, 40, 41,
57
Moslems with blasphemous
thoughts, 111, 112
Mount Sinai Medical School, 115
Murderers, 81
child, *see* Child murderers
mass, *see* Mass murderers

Neuroleptic drugs, 119
Neuropsychologist, 59
Neurotransmitters:
definition, 116–117
dopamine, 119
serotonin, 114, 116–117
Newman Centers, 111

Obsessions, bad thoughts as, 5
Obsessive-compulsive disorder
(OCD), xiv, 57–62
alcohol and drugs and, 60–61
characteristics of, xvi, xvii, 36
cognitive errors of sufferers of,
93–95
cognitive therapy for, *see*
Cognitive therapy
diagnosis of, xvii, 35–36, 131
inability to remember if they've
performed an inappropriate
action, 58
medications for, 13, 14
prevalence of, 36–37
sexual obsessions and, 28

Tourette's syndrome,
relationship to, 55, 59–60
vivid images accompanying bad
thoughts, 61–62
Obsessive-Compulsive
Personality Disorder
(OCPD), 40, 57
characteristics of, 41
OCD, *see* Obsessive-compulsive
disorder (OCD)
O. C. Foundation, 131–32
Olanzapine (Xyprexia), 119
Orap (pimozide), 119
Orbital-frontal cortex, 41, 47–48,
49, 59
effect of alcohol and drugs on,
60
role of, 47–48, 59, 61, 62
Osborne, Ian, 8–9
Overvalued ideas, 109

Pandora, myth of, 8
Paroxetine (Paxil), 116
Past behavior:
as predictor of never acting on
bad thoughts, xiv, 30, 37
violent or sexually
inappropriate, 43–44, 129
Paulist Centers, 111
Pavlov, Ivan, 68
Paxil (paroxetine), 116
Peace of mind, 133
Pedophilia, obsessions of, 76–77
Perfectionism, 94, 133
Perversion, concerns about, 6
Pimozide (Orap), 119
Placebos, 13, 14
Plan of action, 124–36
Playboy, 17
Poe, Edgar Allen, 3–4, 45
Postpartum depression, xiv,
20–23, 51
obsessions about harming
babies during, 20–23, 47

Postpartum depression *(cont'd)*
    SRI drugs and exposure
        therapy to treat, 120–21
Postpartum psychosis, 42–43
Post-traumatic stress disorder
        (PTSD), 62–67, 130
    case example of overlap of bad
        thoughts and, 65–66
    characteristics of, 63
Progress, assessing your, 132–36
Protestants, 111, 112
Prozac (fluoxetine), 116, 120
Psychiatrists, board-certified,
        121–22, 132
Psychopharmacologists, 113, 122

Quality of life:
    goal of improving your, 133
    scale, 133–36
    tracking your progress based
        on, 133–36
Queen Elizabeth Psychiatric
        Hospital, Birmingham, 28
Quetiapine (Seroquel), 119

Rachman, Stanley, 6–8
Racism, fear of, 11
Rape, evolutionary explanation
        for, 46
Rauch, Scott, 57
Relapses, 98–99, 122
Religious people, xv
    cognitive therapy for, 97–105
    fear of damnation, 107–9
    with sexual obsessions,
        exposure therapy for,
        76–78
Religious thoughts, blasphemous,
        xiv, 5, 106–12, 129
    Catholics, 106, 107–9, 111
    exposure therapy for, 87, 88,
        106–11
    Moslems, 111, 112
    Protestants, 111, 112

    SRI drugs to treat, study on,
        115
Risperidone (Risperdal), 119

Sacks, Oliver, 54
Satanic possession, thoughts of,
        82
Savage, Cary, 41, 57, 59–60, 61,
        62
Secrecy about bad thoughts, xv,
        xvii, 22–23, 29–30
    shame leading to, 19, 20, 129
Self-administered therapy:
    assessing your progress, 132–36
    cognitive, 105
    exposure therapy, 89–90,
        128–29, 130–31
    plan of action, 124–36
    using the inventory of bad
        thoughts, 124–28
Selzer, Richard, 137
Sensitivity, *see* Highly sensitive
        people
Seroquel (quetiapine), 119
Serotonin-reuptake inhibiting
        (SRI) drugs, 113–18, 120–21
    see also specific drugs
Sertraline (Zoloft), 116
Sexually abused children, 65–67
Sexual arousal, examining oneself
        for, 10, 35
Sexual thoughts, inappropriate,
        xiv, 5
    about animals, 6, 11, 48, 88–89
    about children, 27–30
    acknowledging without
        suppressing, 17–18
    arousal, examining oneself for,
        10, 35
    case studies, 6, 11–15, 35, 48,
        61, 76–78
    cognitive therapy for, 95–105
    exposure therapy for, 76–78,
        87, 88–89

SRI drugs to treat, study on, 115
Shame, keeping bad thoughts secret due to, 19, 20, 129
Shyness, *see* Highly sensitive people
Smith, Susan, xv, 21, 32–33, 41–42, 46
Socratic questioning technique used in cognitive therapy, 98
Sports Illustrated, 31–32
Spouses, revealing thoughts to, 26
  reactions, 26, 30
Statistics:
  on numbers of people with bad thoughts, xvii, 37
  on obsessive-compulsive disorder, 36–37
  on thoughts of harming children, xvi, 22, 23–24
Stein, Dan, 115
Stelazine (trifluoperazine), 119
Stepparents, 46
Stevenson, Robert Louis, 15–16
Strange Case of Dr. Jekyll and Mr. Hyde, The (Stevenson), 15–16
Sudden infant death (SIDS), 51
Suicide:
  bad thoughts distinguished from suicidal thoughts, 52–53
  contemplating or attempting, xvii, 5–6, 32, 129, 131
Superego, 49, 62
Support groups, xvii, 5, 67, 90
Suppression of bad thoughts, *see* Thought suppression

"Take-home" points, 132
Teenagers, thoughts of harming, 24–25

Therapy, *see* Cognitive therapy; Exposure therapy; Medications
Thérèse of Lisieux, 9
Thioridazine (Mellaril), 119
Thorazine (chlorpromazine), 119
Thought record, 98
Thought suppression, 14–17, 49–51, 69, 93, 98, 129–30
  with drugs or alcohol, 12, 17
  experiment, 99
  factors leading to, 17
Tormenting Thoughts and Secret Rituals (Osborne), 8–9
Totem and Taboo (Freud), 48–49
Tourette's syndrome, 53–57
  characteristics of, 56–57, 59–60, 119
  OCD, relationship to, 55, 59–60
Trains, fears of pushing someone in front of, xvi
Trauma and Recovery: The Aftermath of Violence—from Domestic Abuse to Political Terror (Herman), 63–64, 65, 130
Treatment, xv
  cognitive therapy, *see* Cognitive therapy
  exposure, *see* Exposure therapy
  medication, *see* Medications
  plan of action, 124–36
Tricyclic antidepressants, 120
Trifluoperazine (Stelazine), 119
Twitch and Shout! (Handler), 60

Uncertainty about acting on bad thoughts, 31–37
  fear that the inhibiting functions of the brain won't work, 48
  guilt as positive sign, *see* Guilt, as sign of never acting on bad thoughts

Uncertainty about acting on bad thoughts *(cont'd)*
  inability to guarantee the future, 35
  past behavior, *see* Past behavior, as predictor of never acting on bad thoughts
  trying to attain perfect certainty, 35

Van Oppen, Patricia, 91
Videotapes and audiotapes used in exposure therapy, 80–86, 88–89, 104, 121, 130–31
Violent or aggressive thoughts, inappropriate, xiv, 5
  case studies, 33–34, 78–81
  exposure therapy for, 78–81, 88
Visual images accompanying bad thoughts, 61–62

Warning signs of acting on bad thoughts, 37–44, 128–29

Wegner, Daniel, 14, 49–50
Western Psychiatric Institute and Clinic, Pittsburgh, 23
White Bears and Other Unwanted Thoughts (Wegner), 14, 49–50
"Who's Coaching Your Kid?," 31–32
Wilhelm, Sabine, 92, 95–105
Wisner, Katherine, 20–23, 47, 114, 120
Witztum, Eliezer, 112
World Health Organization (WHO), 74

Xyprexia (olanzapine), 119

Yale-Brown Obsessive Compulsive Scale (YBOCS), 14, 103
Yale University, 55

Zohar, Dr., 55
Zoloft (Sertraline), 116